The HEART of a VAISHNAVA

Exploring the Essence of Humility, Tolerance & Compassion in the Life of God's Servants

PUBLISHED FOR
Bhakti Siddhanta Vani

The HEART of a VAISHNAVA

Exploring the Essence of Humility, Tolerance & Compassion in the Life of God's Servants

HIS HOLINESS SWAMI B.P. PURI

MANDALA
PUBLISHING
SAN RAFAEL

MANDALA
PUBLISHING

17 Paul Drive
San Rafael, CA 94903
t. 415.526.1380
f. 415.532.3281
orders. 800.688.2218
e-mail: info@mandala.org
website: www.mandala.org

ISBN: 1-932771-15-8

Designed *by* Insight Design

Printed *in* Hong Kong
through Palace Press International

Readers interested in the subject
matter may also contact any of the
Gopinath Gaudiya Math branches
in India, located at:

Ishodyan, Sri Mayapur
District Nadia, West Bengal
Phone: 91-3472-245-307

Chakratirtha Road
Jagannath Puri, Orissa
Phone: 91-6752-225-690

Old Dauji Mandhir
Gopeswara Road
Vrindavan, U.P. 281121
Phone: 91-5652-444-185

His Divine Grace
Srila Prabhupada Bhaktisiddhanta Saraswati Thakur

His Holiness Swami B.P. Puri

C O N T E N T S

Introduction

Bhakti Bibudha Bodhayan

It is with great joy that I greet the publication of *The Heart of a Vaishnava*, written by my beloved spiritual master, Om Vishnupada Srila Bhakti Promode Puri Goswami Maharaj. I pray that it will be a source of great joy to devotees everywhere.

Srila Bhakti Promode Puri Maharaj was one of the dearest disciples of Srila Bhaktisiddhanta Saraswati, the great saint who founded the Gaudiya Math, the branches and subbranches of which have now spread around the entire world. We call the Vaishnava family that owes its existence to Saraswati Thakur the Brahma-Madhva-Gaudiya-Saraswata school of Vaishnavism, or sampradaya. My guru personally founded one branch of this family, the Gopinath Gaudiya Math, which has its headquarters in Sri Mayapur Dham, the land of Sri Chaitanya Mahaprabhu's birthplace. His mission, like that of his spiritual master and Chaitanya Mahaprabhu, was to carry aloft the banner of pure devotional service in the modern world.

True Vaishnavas put whatever they preach into practice in their own lives. The problem is that such exemplary Vaishnavas are so very rare in today's world. Srila Puri Maharaj was acutely aware of this shortage of pure practitioners, and so he dedicated himself to preaching and writing articles in order to quell the rising tide of activities that have no foundation in the sacred scriptures and traditions of Vaishnavism. At the same time, he taught and demonstrated how one should go about engaging in the nectar-like activities of pure devotional service.

Most of Puri Maharaj's articles were published over the years in *Chaitanya Vani*, the monthly magazine of the Chaitanya Gaudiya Math, where he was president of the editorial board from its founding in 1961 until 1999, when he entered the eternal pastimes of the Lord. By the efforts of Mandala Publishing, these articles are now being collected, translated into English, and presented in beautifully designed and illustrated editions for the delight of devotees all around the world. To date, Mandala has published several volumes based on these articles, such as *Heart of Krishna* (1995), *Art of Sadhana* (2000) and *Of Love and Separation* (2001). Now this volume, glorifying sadhu sanga or the association of devotees, is happily seeing the light of day. The association of other devotees is the heart of every Vaishnava, for that is what every devotee of Krishna holds most dear.

Who *is a* Vaishnava?

The word Vaishnava is used to designate those who worship Lord Vishnu. In this book, however, it is specifically used to mean the Gaudiya Vaishnavas, who follow in the footsteps of Lord Chaitanya Mahaprabhu and the scripture He held sacred, the Srimad Bhagavatam. The Gaudiya Vaishnavas worship the emperor of joy, Lord Krishna, or, more precisely, the Divine Couple, Sri Sri Radha and Krishna. As such, they should technically be known as "Karshna" (*kārṣṇa*), but they continue nevertheless to use the traditional title Vaishnava.

Swami Bhakti Bibudha Bodhayan

In this world, many so-called religious systems formulating programs for individual and collective peace are constantly coming into existence, but they nearly always teach that we must render service to others on the bodily platform. In this book, however, it is shown that we have to go beyond the gross body and reach the atomic particle of spiritual energy that resides within it, that tiny fragment of the supreme consciousness of God, or Vishnu.

Our constitutional position is that we are tiny sparks of spiritual energy, of consciousness, and are meant to serve the Supreme Consciousness who is present within our hearts.

One way of looking at the Lord's constant presence in the heart is to think of Him as a fire that is lying dormant in wood or any other combustible material. When one rubs two such materials together, such as two sticks, the fire is extracted and becomes apparent.

The first goal of spiritual life is to see the Lord within the heart directly. The Supreme Lord is personally present in His own name. When the individual living entity engages in the chanting of the Holy Name, the process is like rubbing two pieces of wood together and the Lord's presence in his heart becomes clearly manifest, like a spark bursting into flame.

A Vaishnava is one who has experienced the presence of God in this way. He is thus joyous and the fleeting pleasures of this world seem trivial to him. It is thus said that Krishna, makes His home in the Vaishnava's heart. The Holy Name and the Supreme Lord are not different. Therefore, the Vaishnavas, through the worship of His holy names, seat Him in the temple throne of their hearts constantly.

Pure Vaishnavism

In order to achieve this goal, it is necessary to become pure in heart. Saraswati Thakur characterized the pure Vaishnava in the following verse:

kanaka-kāminī, pratiṣṭhā-bāghinī,
chāṛiyache jāre, sei to vaiṣṇava
sei anāsakta, sei śuddha-bhakta,
saṁsār tathā pāy parābhava

One who has abandoned the tigress of money, women and fame is truly a Vaishnava. Such a soul alone is truly detached; such a soul is a pure devotee. The illusory creation of repeated birth and death is defeated before him. *Vaiṣṇava ke? Verse 11*

In other words, Saraswati Thakur says that a pure Vaishnava is one who has transcended bodily concerns and abandoned the desires for material riches, and the company of sensual people who simply fuel the fire of lust, and worldly fame or prestige.

Mahaprabhu's associates, the Goswamis, set the example of abandoning riches and royalty to worship the Supreme Lord, the true sovereign of happiness. Haridas Thakur further showed where true contentment lies by ignoring the direct orders of the magistrate to give up chanting the Holy Name. For this he endured the severe punishment that followed. Pure Vaishnavas follow such examples and constantly repeat the Lord's holy names and thus establish His presence in their hearts.

Krishna *is* without

But the Lord is not uniquely present in the heart. He also resides in His own abode of Goloka.

ānanda-cinmaya-rasa-pratibhāvitābhis
tābhir ya eva nija-rūpatayā kalābhiḥ
goloka eva nivasaty akhilātma-bhūto
govindam ādi-puruṣaṁ tam ahaṁ bhajāmi

I worship Govinda, the primeval Lord, who though present in the hearts of every living creature, resides eternally in His own realm, Goloka, with Radha, resembling His own spiritual figure, the embodiment of the ecstatic potency possessed of the sixty-four artistic activities, in the company of Her con-

> fidantes [sakhis], embodiments of the extensions of Her bodily form, permeated and vitalized by His ever-blissful spiritual rasa. *Brahma-saṁhitā, 5.42*

Goloka is also the natural residence of every single spirit soul. The purpose of human life is to be restored to one's true and eternal identity as an eternal servant of Krishna and to find residence in Goloka—*svarūpe sabāra haya golokete sthiti.*

Every living being without exception is God's eternal servant. It is the servant's duty to render service to his master. The meaning of service is to act for His pleasure. Such service is always transcendental to the body.

Sri Chaitanya Mahaprabhu was Sri Krishna Himself. He became one with Srimati Radharani, His personal internal potency, in order to find the answers to three questions: "What is the glorious nature of Radha's love for Me? What would it be like to relish My own beauty and sweetness through Her eyes?" and "What happiness does She experience through Her love for Me?" By so doing, He demonstrated the glories of Srimati Radharani, who is the source of any capacity anyone has to bring Him joy.

Krishna created Srimati Radharani by manifesting Her out of His own body. In Her turn, She also expands Her body to take on the innumerable forms of the Vraja gopis, or sakhis. She does this in order to better serve Him.

Mahaprabhu's associates and devotees all taught us to serve Krishna by following the leadership of Srimati Radharani. The Gaudiya Vaishnava teaching is thus that we should all serve according to the mood of Srimati Radharani, following in the footsteps of these sakhis, for that is the surest way of bringing Him pleasure.

The secret of the Gaudiya Vaishnava culture of devotional service is that it is not through direct service to Krishna that one achieves success, but through serving those who are dear to Him—culminating with Srimati Radharani and Her potencies, but beginning with the Vaishnavas on this earth, for they are all manifestations of Her power to please Him.

The Vaishnavas demonstrate time and again that their hearts are the nectar-laden inner chamber of service to Krishna and those that He loves. Service to those He loves is an infallible means to please the Lord, and thus of attaining Him. According to the vision of the scriptures, Lord Krishna Himself took human form as Lord Chaitanya to reveal the value of such service.

The Vaishnava universe is one where service in this mood is carried out. If one can attain this genuine happiness, then the forest fire of material life will be extinguished, the father of the universe will be pleased, and so too His devotees, His parts and parcels.

Seeing Krishna *in the* Hearts *of* Others

The Vaishnavas knows the technique of making themselves genuinely and permanently happy, and of bringing this same happiness to others. These are the qualities that we see in the lives of Chaitanya Mahaprabhu's associates like King Prataparudra, Raya Ramananda, Pundarika Vidyanidhi, Rupa Goswami and Sanatan Goswami.

Through their four principal characteristics—humility, tolerance, praise of others and the chanting of the Holy Names—the Vaishnavas control the argumentative mentality of the jivas in this age of Kali and help bring peace to this troubled world.

Those who have adopted the Vaishnava way of life make Lord Krishna, the creator of the universe and fountainhead of all peace and love, the center of their existence. Though service to the Lord is the primary guiding principle of their lives, because they are able to see the Lord present in every living creature's heart, they inevitably show them their due respect. At the same time, they teach them how to see the Lord's presence within themselves and to commit their lives to the service of God.

If we have not learned to love God, it will be impossible for us to truly love our fellow man, what to speak of other creatures. By the same token, if we cannot show compassion for our fellow creatures, whom God has created, is impossible to love Him. As such, it is necessary for everyone to show the proper respect to everyone else, and to love others and God in accordance with the guidelines given in the scripture.

The Vaishnava is thus the nexus of the spiritual and material worlds, of the divine and human. It is possible to see the divine in the Vaishnava, but without the Vaishnava, it is impossible to see the divine.

Puri Maharaj quotes the Lord in this book as saying, "The worship of My devotee is greater than even worship of Me" (*āmāra bhaktera pūjā āmā haite baṛa*). To the non-devotee, this is a puzzle, for Krishna elsewhere says, "The devotee is My heart and I am His." But in *The Heart of a Vaishnava,* Puri Maharaj shows that without the association of devotees, there is no Krishna. The Lord is present in this world through His devotees. If we want to find Krishna, we must look for Him in the midst of Vaishnava association.

This book glorifies the Vaishnava—it tells us of the necessity of Vaishnava association, it tells us how to recognize the Vaishnava, it tells us how to serve the Vaishnava. Indeed, it is the association of Vaishnavas that is most dear to the heart of every other Vaishnava.

Conclusion

The Heart of a Vaishnava is presented in the hope that readers will heed Srila Bhakti Promode Puri Maharaj's pleas to seek out and serve the Vaishnavas, to remain in their company, and to place them in their hearts permanently. This is how they will attain true happiness and will enable them to bring peace back into this world.

Though the subject matter of this book is explained in a simple and endearing manner, it cannot be understood with the intellect alone. It is thus practically impossible for an inexperienced and unqualified individual like myself to grasp it. Nevertheless, I have heard that through the mercy of the spiritual master and the Vaishnavas, even the impossible becomes possible. For this reason, I pray to my spiritual master with all the sincerity at my command that I may serve him and the Vaishnavas birth after birth and thus perfect my existence as a human being.

I would like to offer a special word of thanks and congratulations to my godbrother Sripad Ramdas Prabhu for all the work he has done to bring this volume to the light of day. I ask for our Guru Maharaj to bless him and everyone else at Mandala Publishing so that they may continue this work of publishing these articles in this manner. Books such as this one will bring the greatest benefit to human society. Non-believers will become believers and ordinary people will become capable of imbibing the mercy of the Vaishnavas. So we pray for the continued publication and wide distribution of books like *The Heart of a Vaishnava.*

Praying for the blessings of all the Vaishnavas,

Bhakti Bibudha Bodhayan
President and Acharya
Gopinath Gaudiya Math

The HEART of a VAISHNAVA

CHAPTER 1

Anything Connected *to the* Lord *is* Holy

bhāgavata tulasī gaṅgāya bhakta-jane
caturdhā vigraha kṛṣṇa ei cāri sane
jīva-nyāsa karile śrī-mūrti pūjā haya
janma-mātra e cāri īśvara vede kaya

The Supreme Lord is always associated with the four following entities: the scripture known as the Srimad Bhagavatam, the sacred plant Tulasi Devi, the holy river Ganges, and His devotees. The deity form of the Lord becomes worshipable after it has been consecrated ritually and the Lord's presence has been invoked. Scripture says that these four things, however, are innately divine.

Chaitanya Bhagavata 2.21.81-82

Because of their intimate connection with Him, these four entities have been identified as the Lord's *prakāśa-vigrahas*, or manifestations of the Lord Himself. Although the deity form is generally not considered worshipable until the specific ritual known as *prāṇa-pratiṣṭhā* has been performed, these four *prakāśa-vigrahas* are naturally worshipable—no empowering ritual is needed in order to elevate them to this status. They are all spiritual due to their natural connection to the Lord. The scriptures tell us that though they seem to fall into the category of the "enjoyed," they are in fact the same as the Lord, in the sense that they should be treated as predominators, or enjoyers of the services we render them. They are to always be considered distinct from the predominated material nature and should never be looked upon as potential sources of sense enjoyment.

Srila Prabhupada Bhaktisiddhanta Saraswati explains the above verse as follows:

> Krishna manifests Himself in this world in four forms. On seeing them, one may not immediately recognize them as being the Lord, but one should still worship them, for due to their direct connection to the Lord they are considered to be His manifestations. The name given in Sanskrit to such manifestations is *prakāśa-vigraha*—"the forms by which the Lord appears in the world."
>
> Ordinarily, one has to perform a special ritual consecration known as *prāṇa-pratiṣṭhā* by which one "calls the life" into the Lord's deity form or murti. Prior to such rituals, the Lord's murti remains a mere statue and is not considered worshipable. In the case of the Bhagavatam, Tulasi, the Ganges and the Vaishnava, there is no need for such ritual consecration. Even though one may see them as objects of enjoyment like everything else in the world, they are, in fact, in the position of the enjoyer and so one should engage in their service.
>
> *Gauḍīya-bhāṣya*

The Chaitanya Charitamrita uses the term

tadīya to describe a similar group of four holy objects of worship with a close connection to Krishna—Tulasi Devi, the Vaishnavas, Mathura and the Srimad Bhagavatam.

tadīya tulasī vaiṣṇava
mathurā bhāgavata
ei cārira sevā haya
kṛṣṇera abhimata

The word *tadīya* refers to those things or persons that are connected to the Lord: Tulasi Devi, Krishna's devotees, the land of Mathura, and the Srimad Bhagavatam. Krishna is pleased when one renders service to any of these four.
Chaitanya Charitamrita 2.22.121

This verse comes in the context of the enumeration of sixty-four devotional practices, of which five are considered to be the most important.

sādhu-saṅga nāma-kīrtana
bhāgavata-śravaṇa
mathurā-vāsa śrī-mūrtira
śraddhāya sevana

One should associate with devotees, chant the Holy Name of the Lord, hear Srimad Bhagavatam, reside at Mathura and worship the Deity with faith and reverence. *CC 2.22.214*

Because even a slight performance of any one of these limbs of devotional service awakens love for Krishna, it does not matter whether a person engages in only one or many of them. Clearly, there is a close relationship between these five devotional activities and the concept of *tadīya*, or things related to the Lord.

This book will emphasize that service to the Vaishnavas is inherent in any aspect of devotional service. This is why Srila Narottam Das Thakur sings, *chāḍiyā vaiṣṇava-sevā nistāra pāyeche kebā*—"Who has ever attained the supreme beatitude without serving a Vaishnava?" *Prema-bhakti-candrikā*

The Special Status *of the* Vaishnavas

In two verses from the *Uttara-khaṇḍa* of the *Padma Purana*, Lord Shiva says to Parvati:

ārādhanānāṁ sarveṣāṁ
viṣṇor ārādhanaṁ param
tasmāt parataraṁ devi
tadīyānāṁ samarcanam

Of all the different types of worship, that of Lord Vishnu is best. Even better than the worship of Lord Vishnu is the worship of those things that are connected to Him (*tadīya*).
Bhakti-rasāmṛta-sindhu 1.2.214

arcayitvā tu govindaṁ
tadīyān nārcayet tu yaḥ
na sa bhāgavato jñeyaḥ
kevalaṁ dāmbhikaḥ smṛtaḥ

One who worships Govinda without worshiping those who are connected to Him cannot be considered a true devotee. In fact, he is nothing more than a hypocrite. *Hari-bhakti-vilāsa* 10.362

The Lord does not accept the service of one who has no affection for Tulasi Devi and the other things or persons described as *tadīya*, and who simply tries to show affection for Him alone. The devotees are so dear to Lord Govinda that He subordinates Himself to them. He is therefore easily won over by anyone who shows love and respect for His devotees. Indeed, He says that anyone who professes to be a devotee is not truly His devotee. It is only the person who acts as a devotee of His devotees who can make such a claim:

"Who has ever attained the supreme beatitude without serving a Vaishnava?"

ye me bhakta-janāḥ pārtha
na me bhaktāś ca te janāḥ
mad-bhaktānāṁ ca ye bhaktās
te me bhaktatamā matāḥ

O Arjuna, those who say they are My

devotees are not really My devotees. I only consider those who are the servants of My devotees to be My devotees.
Ādi-purāṇa

When Sri Chaitanya Mahaprabhu observed the affection and esteem in which King Prataparudra held His associate Ramananda Raya, He gave an indication of His intention to be merciful to the King by saying:

prabhu kahe tumi kṛṣṇa-bhakata-pradhāna
tomāke je prīti kare sei bhāgyavān
tomāte je eta prīti haila rājāra
ei guṇe kṛṣṇa tāṅre karibe aṅgīkāra

"My dear Ramananda Raya, you are the foremost of all the devotees of Krishna; therefore, whoever loves you is certainly a very fortunate person. Since the King has shown so much love for you, it is certain that Lord Krishna will accept him." *CC 2.11.26-27*

Uddhava is one of the Lord's foremost devotees. When he approached Krishna in order to learn about the discipline of yoga, the Lord delivered the instructions known as Uddhava Gita (Eleventh Canto, Srimad Bhagavatam). In those instructions, the Lord states the characteristics of a pure devotee:

ādaraḥ paricaryāyāṁ
sarvāṅgair abhivandanam
mad-bhakta-pūjābhyadhikā
sarva-bhūteṣu man-matiḥ

mad-artheṣv aṅga-ceṣṭā ca
vacasā mad-guṇeraṇam
mayy arpaṇaṁ ca manasaḥ
sarva-kāma-vivarjanam

My devotees take great care in rendering service to Me, offering obeisances to Me through the use of all their bodily limbs and faculties. They consider the worship of other devotees to be most important; they see My presence in all living beings. They engage their bodies in working for Me; they use the power of speech for glorifying My qualities. They offer up the activity of the mind to Me, and they give up all material desires. *SB 11.19.21-22*

In his Chaitanya Bhagavata, Vrindavan Das Thakur explains the third line of the first of these verses, *mad-bhakta-pūjābhyadhikā*, as follows:

āmāra bhaktera pūjā āmā haite baḍa
sei prabhu vede bhāgavate kaila daḍha

The Lord has forcefully declared in the Vedas and the Bhagavatam: "Worship of My devotee is even greater than worship of Me." *Cbh 1.1.8*

One must have accumulated many lifetimes of pious acts before being fortunate enough to get the association of a pure devotee. When Vidura's doubts had been erased by listening to Maitreya Muni's explanations of the Supreme Lord, he said in gratitude:

durāpā hy alpa-tapasaḥ
sevā vaikuṇṭha-vartmasu
yatropagīyate nityaṁ
deva-devo janārdanaḥ

One who has made only a few sacrifices and accumulated little merit can never attain service to the travelers on the path to Vaikuntha, great souls who are constantly engaged in glorifying Krishna, God of gods and the controller of all living entities. *SB 3.7.20*

Affection for the Lord awakens as a result of hearing His glories from great souls. As one's affection for the Lord increases, one's identification with the body and bodily activities comes to an end. Therefore, Jagadananda Pandit writes:

sādhu-saṅge kṛṣṇa-nāma ei mātra cāi
saṁsāra jinite āra kono vastu nāi

My only desire is to chant the Holy Name in the company of devotees. I need nothing but this to conquer over the cycle of repeated births and deaths.
Prema-vivarta 6.13

The Pious Merit *that* Results *in the* Association *of* Devotees

The association and guidance of pure devotees is necessary to achieve the state of unmotivated devotional service. Such contact with pure devotees is the fruit of *bhakty-unmukhī sukṛti*, the pious merit that leads to devotion.

bhaktis tu bhagavad-bhakta-
saṅgena parijāyate
sat-saṅgaḥ prāpyate pumbhiḥ
sukṛtaiḥ pūrva-sañcitaiḥ

Devotion is born out of the association with devotees of the Lord. Contact with such saintly persons is given to those who have accumulated pious merit in previous lifetimes. *HBV 10.279*

mahā-prasāde govinde
nāma-brahmaṇi vaiṣṇave
svalpa-puṇyavatāṁ rājan
viśvāso naiva jāyate

Those who have little merit, O king, never develop faith in the Lord's maha prasad, Govinda Himself, the Holy Name (*nāma-brahma*), or the Vaishnavas.
Skānda-purāṇa

At the beginning of his *Bhakti-sandarbha*, Jīva Goswami quotes a verse from the *Brahma-vaivarta Purāṇa* that confirms this very idea:

yāvat pāpais tu malinaṁ
hṛdayaṁ tāvad eva hi
na śāstre satya-buddhiḥ syāt
sad-buddhiḥ sad-gurau tathā

As long as the heart is contaminated by sin, one will not recognize the truths told in the scriptures, nor recognize the genuine spiritual master for who he is.

In other words, one whose heart is filled with sinful desires will not develop faith in the theistic conclusions of the scripture, nor will he recognize the divine authority of the spiritual master. Instead, he takes his gifts and surrenders to a misleader, a guru whose instructions will send him down the road that leads away from Goloka Vaikuntha.

Once Nimi, the king of Videha, fortuitously came upon the nine great devotees known as the Nava Yogendras, who had gathered in his sacrificial arena. Overjoyed to see them, Nimi offered them a respectful greeting appropriate

to their station with the following words:

durlabho mānuṣo deho
dehināṁ kṣaṇa-bhaṅguraḥ
tatrāpi durlabhaṁ manye
vaikuṇṭha-priya-darśanam

ata ātyantikaṁ kṣemaṁ
pṛcchāmo bhavato'naghāḥ
saṁsāre'smin kṣaṇārdho'pi
sat-saṅgaḥ śevadhir nṛṇām

Birth as a human is a very rare achievement for the embodied soul, but I hold that for one having such a short-lived body, it is an even rarer good fortune to just see a devotee who is dear to the Lord of Vaikuntha.

In this world, even a moment's association with saintly persons like yourselves is the greatest treasure attainable by a human being. Therefore, I take this opportunity to ask you sinless souls what is the ultimate good in life. *SB 11.2.29-30*

Only sinless, highly realized devotees like the Nava Yogendras are capable of competently answering submissive inquiries into life's ultimate good (*ātyantika-kṣema*). Such saints have dived deep into the ocean of the scriptures and extracted their essential teachings. With great faith they have applied these teachings in their own lives, and have dedicated themselves to the instruction of others. These are the characteristics of a genuine acharya according to the definition given in the *Vāyu-purāṇa*:

ācinoti yaḥ śāstrārtham
ācāre sthāpayaty api
svayam ācarate yasmād
ācāryas tena kīrtitaḥ

The title of acharya is given to one who has extracted the essential meaning from the scripture, who instills this meaning in the behavior of others, and himself practices what he preaches.

Vāyu-purāṇa

Sri Chaitanya Mahaprabhu was a perfect acharya. Though He is the supremely perfect being, He came into the world to teach by Himself behaving like an exemplary devotee. In Krishna Das Kaviraj's words—*āpani ācari dharma jīvere śikhāya*.

Only through devotion for the spiritual master, who is the Lord's *prakāśa-vigraha*, and for the pure devotees who are fixed up in divine attachment for the Lord, can one fathom the vast ocean of the scriptures and discover their essential teachings. This secret has been immortalized in the following words of the Upanishads:

yasya deve parā bhaktir
yathā deve tathā gurau
tasyaite kathitā hy arthāḥ
prakāśante mahātmanaḥ

Only unto those great souls who have implicit faith in both the Lord and the spiritual master, who is His manifestation and not different from Him, are all the imports of Vedic knowledge automatically revealed.

Śvetāśvatara Upaniṣad 6.23

Without the mercy of the spiritual master one cannot receive the mercy of the Vaishnavas. And without the mercy of both the spiritual master and the Vaishnavas, there is no hope of receiving the Supreme Lord's mercy. The spiritual master gives us the power to recognize the real devotees and separate them from those who simply pretend to be devotees. Without this ability to discriminate, it is easy to fall under the thrall of bad association and be misled from the path of pure devotion.

No one will be able to point us in the direction of genuine devotional association other than a bona fide spiritual master possessing all the qualifications described in scripture: he must be fully conversant in the scriptural truths and enriched by direct realization of the Supreme Truth; he must be free from the pulling and pushing of the material modes and on the highest reaches of the path of bhakti yoga. It is certainly not within the capacity of those who have no real knowledge of Vaishnava doctrine, nor of those who are indifferent to the chanting of the Holy Name, the path of spiritual life instituted by Mahaprabhu Himself. The spiritual master is not one who commits offenses to the Holy Name, nor one who is contaminated by the unholy association of non-devotees, nor is he one engaged in illicit sexual relations.

My only desire is to chant the holy name in the company of devotees. I need nothing but this to conquer over the cycle of repeated births and deaths.
Prema-vivarta 6.13

The blackness of coal cannot be changed by all the water contained in all the lakes and oceans of the world; it can only be transformed into pure white ash by fire. In the same way, it is only through the blazing fire of divine instructions emanating from the Sat Guru that one can be purified of material contamination. Only then can we be freed from the clutches of the witch of material illusion.

bhramite bhramite jadi sādhu-vaidya pāya
tāṅra upadeśa-mantre piśācī palāya
kṛṣṇa-bhakti pāya tabe kṛṣṇa nikaṭe jāya
tāte kṛṣṇa bhaje kare gurura sevana
māyā-jāla chuṭe pāya tabe kṛṣṇera caraṇa

After wandering through the universe in a bewildered condition, if a jiva finds a saintly person to act as exorcist, then the powerful incantation of his teachings overcomes the witch Maya's sorcery and she is forced to run for her life. This fortunate individual then finds pure devotion to Krishna and a place by His side, where he worships Him while continuing to serve the guru's lotus feet. In this way, he is freed from the snares of illusion and attains Krishna.
CC 2.22.14-15, 25

Rupa Goswami was the first to liken the desires for sense gratification and liberation to a witch:

bhukti-mukti-spṛhā yāvat
piśācī hṛdi vartate
tāvad bhakti-sukhāmbodheḥ
katham abhyudayo bhavet

How is it possible for the ocean of devotional happiness to appear in our hearts as long as the witch of desire for sense enjoyment and liberation remains present there? *BRS 1.2.22; CC 2.19.176*

Krishna Das Kaviraj Goswami took further inspiration from Rupa Goswami's idea.

bhukti-mukti-ādi vāñchā jadi mane haya
sādhana karile prema utpanna nā haya

If desires for sense enjoyment and liberation find a place in the heart, all one's culture of devotion will still not result in love for Krishna. *CC 2.19.175*

The desires for bhukti and mukti are here being equated with self-deception and cheating. The Srimad Bhagavatam describes a religious system that is free from any such self-deception, as stated in the introductory verses of the Bhagavatam: *dharmaḥ projjhita-kaitavo'tra paramo nirmatsarāṇāṁ satāṁ* (SB 1.1.2). Although all the four objects of human life are considered to be *kaitava*, or self-deception arising out of ignorance, the desire for liberation is the deepest darkness of all, for it can completely eradicate any gain one makes on the path of devotion.

Sridhar Swami, in his purports to Srimad Bhagavatam, explains the words *projjhita-kaitava* in the following way: "The prefix *pra-* indicates that the desire for liberation has been completely repudiated" (*pra-śabdena mokṣābhisandhir api nirasta iti*).

On this basis, the purity of devotion is measured by the extent to which one is free of desire for sense gratification and liberation, or the four goals of life: religiosity, material achievements, sense enjoyment and salvation. Elsewhere, Krishna Das Kaviraj Goswami speaks of all auspicious or inauspicious actions (*śubhāśubha-karma*) as being the darkness of ignorance that interferes with the attainment of bhakti (CC 1.1.94). Thus the words of this introductory Bhagavata verse lead us to the definition of pure devotion given by Rupa Goswami : It is free of any desire other than the pleasure of the Lord (*anyābhilāṣitā-śūnyam*). The causeless mercy of Gaura Nitai results in the destruction of all such ignorant self-deception and allows the knowledge of pure devotion to rise like the sun in the darkness.

Although all the four objects of human life are considered to be self-deception arising out of ignorance, the desire for liberation is the deepest darkness of all.

The essence of the three categories of spiritual knowledge—sambandha, abhidheya and prayojana—is Krishna, devotional service to Krishna, and love for Krishna, respectively.

kṛṣṇa bhakti haya abhidheya pradhāna
bhakti mukha nirīkṣaka karma-yoga-jñāna

> The foremost practice leading to the supreme goal of life (abhidheya) is devotional service to Krishna. All other spiritual practices, the path of works, self-discipline or philosophical speculation, all look to bhakti for their completion.
> *CC 2.22.17*

Amongst the various practices of devotional service, the chanting of the Holy Names has pride of place. The scriptures are thus full of glorifications of the association of devotees, sat sanga, without which one may chant for thousands of lifetimes and still not attain love for Krishna:

sādhu saṅga kṛpā kiṁ vā kṛṣṇera kṛpāya
kāmādi-duḥsaṅga chāḍi śuddha-bhakti pāya

> Either through the benediction of devotional association or through the mercy of Krishna Himself, one is freed of the bad association resulting from lust, anger and greed, and attains pure devotional service. *CC 2.24.97*

sat-saṅgān mukta-duḥsaṅgo
hātuṁ notsahate budhaḥ
kīrtyamānaṁ yaśo yasya
sakṛd ākarṇya rocanam

> Once freed from bad association by keeping the company of the saintly, an intelligent person becomes reluctant to give up listening to the glories of the Lord, which bring so much joy, even if heard only once. *SB 1.10.11*

Jagadananda Pandit thus advises us to pray for devotional association in order to be able to perfect our chanting of the Holy Name:

asādhu-saṅgete bhāi nāma nāhi haya

nāmākṣara bāhirāya baṭe nāma kabhu naya
kabhu nāmābhāsa sadā haya nāmāparādha
e saba jānibe bhāi kṛṣṇa-bhaktir bādha
yadi karibe kṛṣṇa-nāma sādhu-saṅga kara
bhukti-mukti-siddhi-vāñchā dūre parihara

O brother! You cannot chant the Holy Name in the association of non-devotees. The sounds of the Holy Name may come out of your mouth, but this will not really be the Name. It will sometimes be the Name's reflection (*nāmābhāsa*) and sometimes offensive chanting (*nāmāparādha*), but brother, you should know that in either case, this kind of chanting impedes the attainment of pure devotion to Krishna. If you truly want to chant the Holy Names, then associate with pure devotees and keep the desires for sense enjoyment, liberation and yogic powers at bay.
Prema-vivarta 7.1-3

The Four Kinds *of* People Who Turn *to the* Lord

In Bhagavad Gita, Krishna mentions four reasons that motivate people to turn to God: distress, ambition, curiosity and wisdom. In his discussion of this topic, Krishna Das Kaviraj Goswami divides these four into two categories. He classifies the distressed and the ambitious seeker of wealth or other material rewards as *bubhukṣu* ("desirers of sense gratification") and the curious and the wise as *mumukṣu* ("desirers of liberation"). But one who has accumulated the necessary piety soon comes to abandon all desires, knowing that they hold him back from pure devotion.

ārta arthārthī dui sa-kāma bhitare gaṇi
jijñāsu jñānī dui mokṣa-kāmī māni
ei cāri sukṛti haya mahā-bhāgyavān
tat-tat-kāmādi chāḍi haya śuddha-bhaktimān

The distressed and the seeker of wealth are both counted as devotees with material desires, whereas the curious and the learned harbor the desire for liberation. Though all four kinds of devotees are highly fortunate and pious, it is only when they transcend their desires that they become pure devotees.
CC 2.24.90-91

Whereas Krishna Das Kaviraj called these desires "cheating" (*kaitava*) and "the darkness of ignorance" (*andha-tamaḥ*) in the first chapter of the Chaitanya Charitamrita, in this context (*Madhya-līlā* 24.94) he characterizes them as "wicked association" (*duḥsaṅga*), as well as "self-deception" (*ātma-vañcanā*). The idea is that anyone who makes a pretense of engaging in devotion while remaining motivated by other desires not only deceives himself but others as well. Anyone who is a cheater or who tolerates such cheating behavior is by definition *duḥsaṅga* or bad association. Contact with such persons will render even long-term dedication to the practice of bhakti futile. Thus the Bhagavatam advises:

> *O brother! You cannot chant the Holy Name in the association of non-devotees.*

tato duḥsaṅgam utsṛjya
satsu sajjeta buddhimān
santa evāsya chindanti
mano-vyāsaṅgam uktibhiḥ

An intelligent person should abandon all bad association and hold fast to the company of devotees. Such saints are the only ones who, by their instructions, can cut through our unhealthy mental attachments. *SB 11.26.26*

In an important verse in the Bhagavatam, Lord Kapila Deva instructs his mother Devahuti in the gradual development of faith beginning with the association of devotees and hearing Krishna conscious topics from them. Faith means taking up the practice of disciplined devotional activity. Once we begin such practice, our inner life develops as far as *rati* or *bhāva*, the stage of devotional feeling, and goes on from there to devotion in its purest state, or *prema*.

satāṁ prasaṅgān mama vīrya-saṁvido
bhavanti hṛt-karṇa-rasāyanāḥ kathāḥ
taj-joṣaṇād āśv apavarga-vartmani

śraddhā ratir bhaktir anukramiṣyati

My heroic pastimes, when heard in the association of pure devotees, are very pleasing to the ear and satisfying to the heart. As a result of joyfully relishing these pastimes in such association, one quickly advances on the path of liberation, passing through the stages of faith (*śraddhā*), the revelation of one's divine relationship with Krishna (*rati*), and true love for Him (*bhakti*). *SB 3.25.25*

In discussing the need to seek out like-minded association, Rupa Goswami quotes the following verse from *Hari-bhakti-sudhodaya* (8.51), in which Hiranyakashipu tells Prahlada that one's own character reflects the company he keeps:

yasya yat-saṅgatiḥ puṁso
maṇivat syāt sa tad-guṇaḥ
sva-kula-rddhyai tato dhīmān
sva-yūthān eva saṁśrayet

Like a mirror, a person takes on the qualities of those with whom he comes into contact. One who is intelligent should therefore seek the company of more advanced persons who share the same ideals, in order to cultivate their good qualities in himself. *BRS 1.2.229*

A *lava* is equal to 4/45th of a second, or the time that it takes to blink. It is said that even as little as a *lava's* time of association with advanced devotees will result in the attainment of all perfections. This is the potency of the fellowship of devotees as glorified by Krishna Das Kaviraj:

sādhu-saṅga sādhu-saṅga sarva śāstra kaya
lava mātra sādhu-saṅge sarva siddhi haya

All the scriptures repeatedly glorify the association of the saintly. A mere moment's association with the saintly results in all perfection. *CC 2.22.54*

What are the benefits of making friendship with the saintly? Their compassion—that is, of the guru and the pure devotees—principally results in the dissipation of our bad habits and the development of pure bhakti.

kṛṣṇa-bhakti-janma-mūla haya sādhu-saṅga
kṛṣṇa-prema janme teṅho punaḥ mukhya aṅga

The root cause of devotional service to Lord Krishna is association with advanced devotees; nevertheless, even after one's dormant love for Krishna has awakened, such association remains the main pillar of a devotee's spiritual life.
CC 2.22.80

mahat-kṛpā vinā kona karme bhakti naya
kṛṣṇa-bhakti dūre rahu saṁsāra nahe kṣaya

Without the favor of a great devotee, no activity qualifies as devotion. Not only are we unable to attain pure devotion to Krishna, but we cannot even be freed from the bondage of material existence.
CC 2.22.51

Bhakti *is the* Only Fully Independent Spiritual Path

Different kinds of piety lead either to sense gratification or to liberation. According to the kinds of meritorious deeds performed in this or earlier lives, we come into contact with exemplary individuals on one of the various paths of religious or spiritual advancement. If these guides or companions are on the path of karma or liberation, however, the result will only be increasing desires for these particular goals. On the other hand, the pious merit that leads to devotion gives access to an encounter with a Vaishnava and, through his or her association, to pure devotion. But it must be pointed out again that the path of works and the path of knowledge cannot even give their own professed results without the help of bhakti, whereas bhakti is completely independent. Bhakti needs no help whatsoever from karma or jnana to give the unequalled prize of love of Godhead. The supreme goal of human life, prema, can only be achieved by the exclusive practice of devotion, consisting of hearing and chanting about Krishna.

The Supreme Lord has stated this with great clarity in the Srimad Bhagavatam:

tasmān mad-bhakti-yuktasya
yogino vai mad-ātmanaḥ
na jñānaṁ na ca vairāgyaṁ
prāyaḥ śreyo bhaved iha
yat karmabhir yat tapasā
jñāna-vairāgyataś ca yat
yogena dāna-dharmeṇa
śreyobhir itarair api
sarvaṁ mad-bhakti-yogena
mad-bhakto labhate'ñjasā
svargāpavargaṁ mad-dhāma
kathañcid yadi vāñchati

na kiñcit sādhavo dhīrā
bhaktā hy ekāntino mama
vāñchanty api mayā dattaṁ
kaivalyam apunar-bhavam

For the devoted yogi who has surrendered his thoughts to Me, neither knowledge nor renunciation are considered to be the sources of true good in this world. All the results obtained through ritual practices, penance, philosophy, renunciation, yogic discipline, charity or diligent execution of one's prescribed duties, or any other method of self-improvement, are easily had by My devotees through the practice of devotional service to Me alone. My saintly, patient and single-minded devotees desire none of this; yet I still bestow these rewards on them, up to and including liberation and freedom from rebirth.

SB 11.20.31-34

All religious activities other than devotional service to the Supreme Lord are thus like the teats on the neck of a goat—they ultimately serve no worthwhile function.

ata eva māyā-moha chāḍi buddhimān
nitya-tattva kṛṣṇa-bhakti karena sandhāna

Therefore an intelligent person gives up his enchantment with this illusory material world and searches out the eternal truth of devotion to Krishna.

Kalyāna Kalpa Taru

Pious people or sadhus on the karma and jnana paths are never characterized as *tadīya*, "people or things related to the Lord." Thus, a person who is attempting to advance in the discipline of bhakti must be especially careful about the type of person to whom he renders service. Otherwise, he will not master the discipline and attain its goal: perfection in pure devotion and love for Krishna.

The Supreme Lord, Chaitanya Mahaprabhu, says:

bhajanera madhye śreṣṭha nava-vidhā bhakti
kṛṣṇa-prema kṛṣṇa dite dhare mahā-śakti

tāra madhye sarva-śreṣṭha nāma-saṅkīrtana
niraparādhe laile nāma pāya prema-dhana

> Of the many ways of executing devotional service, nine are considered to be the best, for they possess the greatest capacity to deliver love for Krishna and thus Krishna Himself. Of these nine processes of devotional service, the most important is the chanting of the Lord's Holy Name, for if one chants without committing offenses he will obtain the treasure of love for the Lord. *CC 3.4.70-1*

Freedom from offenses is the key ingredient to attaining Krishna prema, and such freedom is not found through any method other than taking shelter of the Holy Name. Bhakti can bestow upon its practitioners all the results of worldly enjoyment and salvation independent of any other discipline. If one chants the Holy Names tirelessly, the Name itself will bestow its grace. By eliminating all offenses, one achieves the capacity to chant without end, qualifying one for the great prize of prema. As long as one remains tolerant of offenses or carelessly continues to commit them, there is no possibility of attaining prema.

By eliminating all offenses, one achieves the capacity to chant without end, qualifying one for the great prize of prema.

The Grace *of* Krishna *and the* Vaishnavas Erases Other Desires

The Bhagavatam advises everyone, regardless of their motivation, to engage in devotional service to the Lord.

akāmaḥ sarva-kāmo vā
mokṣa-kāma udāra-dhīḥ
tīvreṇa bhakti-yogena
yajeta puruṣaṁ param

> Whether one desires everything or nothing, or whether one desires to merge into the existence of the Lord, he is intelligent only if he worships Lord Krishna, the Supreme Personality of Godhead, by intensely rendering Him transcendental loving service. *SB 2.3.10*

Vishwanath Chakravarti interprets the word *tīvreṇa* ("intensely") as meaning an engagement in transcendental loving service without any admixture of karma or jnana practices.[1] The power of even basic devotional acts is such that one can be liberated by them.

kṛṣṇa tomāra haṅa jadi
bale eka-bāra
māyā-bandha haite kṛṣṇa
tāre kare pāra

> If someone says just once to Krishna, "I am yours," then Krishna delivers him from his bondage to the illusory energy. *CC 2.22.33*

The Supreme Lord Ramachandra made this same assurance when telling Sugriva about His meeting with Vibhishan:

sakṛd eva prapanno yas
tavāsmīti ca yācate
abhayaṁ sarvadā tasmai
dadāmy etad vrataṁ mama

> It is My promise that if someone truly surrenders to Me and says just once, "I am yours," then I grant him fearlessness for all eternity. *CC 2.22.34*

Bhakti transforms a devotee, even if he is motivated by other kinds of desires, because the external acts of devotion attract Krishna's mercy. This is explained by Krishna Das Kaviraj Goswami:

bhukti-mukti-siddhi-kāmī subuddhi jadi haya
gāḍha-bhakti-yoge tabe kṛṣṇere bhajaya
anya-kāmī jadi kare kṛṣṇera bhajan
nā māgiteha kṛṣṇa tāre dena sva-caraṇ
kṛṣṇa kahe āmā bhaje māge viṣaya-sukha
amṛta chāḍi viṣa māge ei baṛa mūrkha
āmi vijña ei mūrkhe viṣaya kene dibo
sva-caraṇāmṛta diyā viṣaya bhulāibo

When those who desire material hap-

piness, liberation, or mystic powers actually become intelligent, they take to Krishna consciousness by engaging in intense devotional service to Lord Sri Krishna. If those who desire material enjoyment or merging into the existence of the Absolute Truth engage in the Lord's transcendental loving service, they will immediately attain shelter at Krishna's lotus feet, even though they did not ask for it. Krishna is therefore very merciful. Krishna says, "If one engages in My transcendental loving service, but at the same time wants the opulence of material enjoyment, he is very, very foolish. Indeed, he is just like a person who gives up ambrosia to drink poison. Since I know what is of true benefit to him, why should I give this fool material prosperity? Instead I will induce him to drink the nectar of My lotus feet and make him forget all illusory material enjoyment."

CC 2.22.35, 37-39

The above series of verses from the Chaitanya Charitamrita has been paraphrased by Srila Bhaktivinode Thakur in his *Amṛta-pravāha-bhāṣya* as follows:

As a result of bad character and bad association, a living entity develops desires for sense enjoyment, liberation or mystic powers. If by some chance he comes into contact with pure devotees, he can develop the clear intelligence to abandon all desire for such things. Those who desire sensual pleasures, salvation or mystic prowess are bereft of any desire for pure devotion. Nevertheless, if out of some good fortune they come to engage in the recognized practices of pure devotion, then Krishna is so merciful that He will bestow prema upon them, even if that was not their original objective. Krishna says to Himself, "This person was seeking something else, but even so has been engaged in My service. Nevertheless, something of the lower nature still infects his heart. He has given up the nectarean cup of prema and wants to drink from a chalice of poison, which demonstrates how foolish he is. His inability to pray for the nectar of immortality is a sign of his ignorance. By contrast, I am both wise and experienced. I know what he needs in order to perfect his life, so I will give him a taste of the nectar of My lotus feet. This ecstasy will make him forget forever the bitter taste of material pleasures."

Once the demigods were glorifying the land of India, saying that it was the gateway to the spiritual world, and that a human birth there was the summit of good fortune and a necessary prerequisite to attaining the Lord's abode, for the Supreme Lord Hari takes birth amongst the humans of this land just to give them a taste of His ambrosial pure devotional service. While thus singing the praises of a human birth in the land of India, the demigods remarked on the nature of the Lord's mercy:

satyaṁ diśaty arthitam arthito nṛṇāṁ
naivārthado yat punar arthitā yataḥ
svayaṁ vidhatte bhajatām anicchatām
icchā-pidhānaṁ nija-pāda-pallavam

It is true that Lord Krishna fulfills one's desire whenever someone petitions Him to do so. However, He does not award anything that, once having been received, will be asked for again and again. He thus personally bestows His lotus feet on those who worship Him, whereby they will forget all their passing material desires, even if that was not what they thought they wanted. *SB 5.19.27*

kāma lāgi kṛṣṇe bhaje pāya kṛṣṇa-rase
kāma chāḍi dāsa haite haya abhilāṣe

Someone who engages in Lord Krishna's devotional service out of some base motivation acquires instead a taste to serve Him. As a result he gives up his material desires and longs to become the Lord's eternal servant. *CC 2.22.41*

According to Bhaktivinode Thakur, "If someone has the good fortune to come into the association of devotees and yet only takes up devotional service to Krishna as a means of achieving some selfish mundane purpose, he still soon realizes that these objectives are of little value. This comes about as a result of the higher taste experienced from bhakti. Krishna worship is so pure and holy a thing that anyone who comes into contact with it soon rejects his other desires and seeks to become a servant of the Lord." *Amṛta-pravāha-bhāṣya*

This power of devotional service to make one forget one's material desires was demonstrated by the great child devotee Dhruva when he refused the boons personally offered by the Supreme Lord, saying:

sthānābhilāṣī tapasi sthito'haṁ
tvāṁ prāptavān deva-munīndra-guhyam
kācaṁ vicinvann api divya-ratnaṁ
svāmin kṛtārtho'smi varaṁ na yāce

O my Lord, I took up the practice of penance and austerities out of a wish to become a great ruler. Now that I have attained You, who remain hidden to even great demigods, saintly persons and kings, I feel like someone who finds a most valuable jewel while looking for only some fragments of broken glass. I am now so fulfilled that I am left with no benediction to pray for.
Hari-bhakti-sudhodaya 7.28

Bhaktisiddhanta Saraswati Thakur comments in his *Anubhāṣya*, "The association of pure devotees, Krishna's mercy and devotion to Krishna share this common characteristic: they rid one of all taste for the company of non-devotees, or for any good fortune arising from the illusory energy, as well as any tendency to take up the paths of karma, jnana and yoga." *CC 2.24.99*

Bhakti Destroys the Desire for Liberation

Krishna Das Kaviraj Goswami further demonstrates the power of bhakti to eradicate the desire for mukti by citing the examples of Shukadeva, the four Kumaras and the nine Yogendras. From his very birth, Shukadeva was absorbed in the knowledge of the impersonal Brahman concept of the Divine. By the grace of his father, Vyasa, he was attracted to the qualities of the personal form of the Lord. He then took instruction in the Srimad Bhagavatam from Vyasa and attained a taste for Krishna's pastimes.

The four Kumaras inhaled the delightful aroma of Tulasi leaves that had been offered to Lord Narayan's lotus feet and immediately forgot their attachment for the impersonal Brahman. Their self-satisfaction in spiritual knowledge disappeared when their minds and bodies became agitated with ecstatic reactions.

The nine great yogis known as the Nava Yogendras had been cultivating spiritual knowledge from childhood. Nevertheless, when they heard the Lord's glories being sung by Lord Brahma, Shiva and Narada, they were also attracted to His qualities and began to engage in His devotional service. All these examples of liberated souls being attracted by the qualities of the Lord give weight to the claim of Suta Goswami, who told the sages at Naimisharanya:

> Lord Hari takes birth amongst the humans of this land, just to give them a taste of His ambrosial pure devotional service.

ātmārāmāś ca munayo
nirgranthā apy urukrame
kurvanty ahaitukīṁ bhaktim
ittham-bhūta-guṇo hariḥ

The many types of *ātmārāmas* all take pleasure in the Self in one way or another. Though already free from all material bonds, they still engage in causeless devotional service unto the Lord who performs glorious feats. Truly, the Lord possesses transcendental qualities and is therefore able to attract everyone, including liberated souls. *SB 1.7.10*

This power inherent in bhakti may act through any of the aforementioned five devotional activities.

sat-saṅga kṛṣṇa-sevā bhāgavata nāma
vraje vāsa ei pañca sādhana pradhāna
ei pañca madhye eka svalpa yadi haya
subuddhi janera haya kṛṣṇa-premodaya
udāra mahatī jāṅra sarvottamā buddhi
nānā kāme bhaje tabu pāya bhakti-siddhi
bhakti-prabhāva sei kāma chāṛāñā
kṛṣṇa-pade bhakti karāya guṇe ākarṣiyā

The five most powerful processes of devotional service are association with devotees, serving Lord Krishna's deity form, hearing the Srimad Bhagavatam, chanting the Holy Names, and residing in Vraja Dham. If an intelligent person comes into even minimal contact with any one of these five types of devotional practice, his dormant love for Krishna is awakened. One who has this kind of broad, deep and superior intelligence serves the Lord even if he has some motive, with the result that he eventually attains the perfection of devotion. The power of devotion is such that it makes him give up all material desires and, by attracting him to the transcendental qualities of the Lord, bestows on him devotion to Krishna's feet.

CC 2.24.187-188, 190,192

Ultimately, Devotion Must Be Exclusive

Srila Krishna Das Kaviraj Goswami also names these five principal devotional activities again in the twenty-second chapter of the *Madhya-līlā*. There he mentions that without determined and faithful adherence to them, one cannot expect the fruit of love of Godhead to ripen on the vine of devotion. In this connection, Kaviraj Goswami also describes symptoms of superior intelligence: one who gives up both gross and subtle sense gratification and dedicates himself to the satisfaction of Krishna's senses is truly intelligent. True love for Krishna has absolutely no element of self-directed sensual desire. If one has come to this understanding, then he deserves the title *udāra-dhī*, as mentioned in the Bhagavatam verse quoted above: "Whether one desires everything or nothing, or whether he desires to merge into the existence of the Lord, he is intelligent only if he worships Lord Krishna, the Supreme Personality of Godhead, by intensely rendering transcendental loving service." (SB 2.3.10)

Without exercising such discrimination, one will be unable to distinguish pure devotional service from other kinds of devotional activity that are sullied by philosophical speculation or the admixture of some other motivation. He or

she will thus end up mistaking ignorance for wisdom and sectarianism for liberalism. Like so many others in this material world, one will be misled and think that any spiritual path is just as good as another—*jata mata tata patha*. In fact, there is only one way to reach Goloka Vrindavan, the abode of Krishna. That path is known as bhakti yoga. This has been made clear both in the Gita and the Bhagavatam.

True love for Krishna has absolutely no element of self-directed sensual desire.

This kind of exclusiveness is also described in *Gītā-māhātmya*, a short hymn in glorification of the Bhagavad Gita that is to be sung before studying or reciting it:

ekaṁ śāstraṁ devakī-putra-gītam
eko devo devakī-putra eva
eko mantras tasya nāmāni yāni
karmāpy ekaṁ tasya devasya sevā

There is only one scripture—the one that was sung by the Son of Devaki.
There is only one God—the one who is known as the Son of Devaki.
There is only one hymn to be sung—the names of the Son of Devaki.
We have only one duty—to serve this one supreme God.

We can attain prema only through exclusive devotion to Krishna. Such exclusive devotion comes about through contact with Krishna's pure devotees, who know nothing other than Him.

CHAPTER 2

Mahaprabhu Worshiped Those *who are* Dear *to the* Lord

Sri Chaitanya Mahaprabhu is the spiritual master of the three spheres of existence. He set the example of how to act as a devotee and, in so doing, showed how to serve those who are close to Krishna—the Vaishnavas, the holy Tulasi plant, the Ganges River and Maha Prasad. When staying in Puri Dham, Kashi Mishra would bring Lord Jagannath's flower garlands to Mahaprabhu. Mahaprabhu is Narayan, the teacher of all the worlds, yet when He accepted this prasadam, He treated it with what Vrindavan Das Thakur described as *mahā-bhaya-bhakti*—"devotion mixed with great fear."

When a person enters the fourth stage of human life, sannyas, then he is offered respect by everyone as a matter of etiquette. As a general principle, those in the renounced order of life are worshipable by all other divisions of human society and even a sannyasi's own father must bow down to him. Mahaprabhu was such a sannyasi, yet He set the example for all of us by prostrating Himself before every Vaishnava that He met. The Vaishnava is therefore on the highest rung of human society.

TULASI DEVI

As far as Tulasi Devi is concerned, Vrindavan Das describes how Sri Caitanya Mahaprabhu served this plant so beloved of Krishna—

tulasīra bhakti ebe śuna mana diyā
je rūpe kailena līlā tulasī laiyā
eka kṣudra-bhāṇḍe divya mṛttikā pūriyā
tulasī dekhena sei ghaṭe āropiyā
prabhu bole – āmi tulasīre nā dekhile
bhāla nāhi bāsoṅ jena matsya bine jale
jabe cale saṅkhyā nāma kariyā grahaṇa
tulasī laiyā agre cale eka-jana
paścāte calena prabhu tulasī dekhiyā
paṛaye ānanda-dhārā śrī-aṅga bahiyā
saṅkhyā-nāma laite je sthāne prabhu baise
tathā-i rākhena tulasīre prabhu pāśe
tulasīre dekhena japena saṅkhyā nāma
e bhakti-yogera tattva ke bujhibe āna
punaḥ sei saṅkhyā-nāma sampūrṇa kariyā
calena īśvara saṅga tulasī laiyā

Now listen carefully to the Lord's pastimes with Tulasi Devi and how He devoted Himself to her. One day, He filled a small pot with the richest soil and transplanted a tulasi plant in it, saying, "If I don't see Tulasi Devi, I feel uninspired, like a fish deprived of water."

Whenever the Lord chanted japa, counting the Holy Names, one of His devotees would walk in front of Him, carrying the tulasi plant. The Lord would follow, meditating on Tulasi Devi, His entire body awash with ecstatic symptoms. When the Lord chanted japa sitting down, then His servant would place Tulasi Devi beside Him and the Lord would chant while gazing on her. Can anyone understand fully the Lord's devotional practice?

Even after the Lord had finished chanting His japa for the day, a servant carrying Tulasi Devi would follow Him wherever he went.

śikṣā guru nārāyaṇa je karāyena śikṣā
tāhā je mānaye sei jana pāya rakṣā

Mahaprabhu is Lord Narayan, the teacher of all the worlds. One who follows His teachings and example will be delivered.
Cbh 3.8.154-62

Srila Bhaktisiddhanta Saraswati Prabhupada writes in his commentary to this passage: "Mahaprabhu demonstrated the special position of Tulasi Devi for the benefit of all those who think her to be an ordinary shrub. Tulasi Devi is beloved of Keshava Krishna and is 'His' (*tadīya*). Anyone who tries to attain service to Krishna while circumventing those who are beloved of Him will meet with failure. In this connection, one should remember that the Lord says that anyone who worships Him without worshiping His devotees is nothing more than a hypocrite and cannot be considered a true devotee."
Cbh 3.8.159, Gauḍīya-bhāṣya

When Mahaprabhu was still a householder in Nabadwip, His daily schedule included bathing in the Ganges with the other devotees, changing into clean clothes, returning home and washing His feet on entering there. He would then water Tulasi Devi, circumambulate and bow down to her. Next, He would go into the temple to worship the Deity, after which He would circumambulate the temple while reciting prayers. His worship would conclude with offering the bhoga that had been prepared and decorated with tulasi flowers by Sachi Devi. Then the Lord would sit down and partake of prasad Himself.

vastra parivarta kari dhuilā caraṇa
tulasīre jala diyā karilā secana
yathā vidhi kari prabhu govinda pūjana
āsiyā vasilā gṛhe karite bhojana
tulasīra mañjarī sahita divya anna
māye āni sammukhe karilā upasanna
viśvaksenere tabe kari nivedana
ananta-brahmāṇḍa nātha karena bhojana

The Lord changed His clothes and washed His feet. He then watered Tulasi Devi. Then, after worshiping Govinda Deva according to the rules, He went to sit in the house to eat. His mother came with a delicious meal decorated with tulasi flowers and placed it before Him. Mahaprabhu, the Lord of the unlimited universes, offered the prasadam to the Lord's associate Vishwaksen and then commenced eating Himself.
Cbh 2.1.187-190

In his commentaries, Srila Bhaktisiddhanta Saraswati Thakur writes:

"Anyone who has received initiation in the Vaishnava mantras is obliged to engage in regular worship of the Deity, including offering all he eats to the Lord. When devotees make such food offerings, they should remember to place tulasi leaves or flowers on them because Lord Vishnu does not accept any food without tulasi. Tulasi is most beloved of Lord Krishna and thus her leaves and flowers are also most dear to Him. The term *vārkṣārcāvatāra*, meaning the Lord's incarnation meant for accepting worship (*arcāvatāra*) in the form of a tree (*vārkṣa*),

Tulasi Devi is most beloved of Lord Krishna and thus her leaves and flowers are also most dear to Him.

is applied to Tulasi Devi. Her leaves and flowers are therefore prescribed as an essential part of the worship of the Lord's other *arcāvatāra*, i.e., the deity form of the Lord in the temple. These regulations are found in all the scriptural texts that describe the procedures by which one is to worship such deity forms of the Lord.

Lord Gauranga set the example of worshiping Tulasi Devi by watering her. Then after completing that act of worship, He would go on to perform the puja of His household deity Govinda, the Shalagram stone that had been worshiped in the family for generations. The procedure followed by Mahaprabhu is the ideal that every pious householder should try to emulate. In this way, all householders should take up the daily puja of the Lord's deity form and only eat the remnants of offerings made to this deity, honoring them with great faith and humility.
Cbh 2.1.187-8, Gauḍīya-bhāṣya

In the ninth chapter of *Hari-bhakti-vilāsa*, a great amount of material is cited glorifying Tulasi Devi, praising the benefits of eating tulasi leaves, and so on. Nevertheless, no Vaishnava will eat tulasi leaves or flowers without first having offered them to Krishna.

śrīmat-tulasyāḥ patrasya
māhātmyaṁ yadyapīdṛśam
tathāpi vaiṣṇavais tan na
grāhyaṁ kṛṣṇārpaṇaṁ vinā

Though the glories of the tulasi leaf are as great as this, no Vaishnava will accept one unless it has first been offered to Krishna. *HBV 9.227*

Mahaprabhu is the Supreme Lord Himself, yet He accepted the mood and character of a devotee to set the example of how to live the life of devotion. In this particular case, He showed through the worship of Tulasi Devi how one should honor the persons and things that are close to the Lord.

Vishwaksen

In the above section from the Chaitanya Bhagavata, Vrindavan Das also mentions that the Lord offered Govinda's prasadam to Vishwaksen before eating Himself. Srila Bhaktisiddhanta Saraswati Prabhupada gives the following details about Vishwaksen:

Vishwaksen (*viśvaksena* or *viṣvaksena*) is an eternal associate of Vishnu; he has a four-armed form and always wears the remnants of the Lord's garlands and raiments. In the *Hari-bhakti-vilāsa* (8.209-217), it is said that one should offer a one hundredth part of the Lord's remnants to this personality, *viśvaksenāya dātavyaṁ naivedyaṁ tac-chatāṁśakam.*
Cbh 2.1.190, Gauḍīya-bhāṣya

Vishwaksen is also mentioned in the Srimad Bhagavatam—

durgāṁ vināyakaṁ vyāsaṁ
viṣvaksenaṁ gurūn surān
sve sve sthāne tv abhimukhān
pūjayet prokṣaṇādibhiḥ

One should worship Durga, Ganesh, Vyasa Deva, Vishwaksen, all one's gurus and the gods by sprinkling water on each in their proper place. *SB 11.27.29*

dattvācamanam uccheṣaṁ
viṣvaksenāya kalpayet
mukha-vāsaṁ surabhimat
tāmbūlādyam athārhayet

After offering the Lord water to wash the mouth and hands, one should offer the Lord's remnants to Vishwaksen, and then offer a pleasantly scented mouth purifier such as tambula. *SB 11.27.43*

Sridhar Swami comments on the latter verse in his *Bhāvārtha-dīpikā* as follows:

tatra ubhayatra bhagavato
bhojana-samāptiṁ dhyātvā
ācamanaṁ dattvā uccheṣaṁ
viṣvaksenāya kalpayitvā

tad-anujñayā paścāt svayaṁ bhuñjīta.

> The scriptures ordain that after one has completed meditating on the Lord's taking His meal, one should offer Him water to wash His hands and mouth. The devotee should then mentally offer the Lord's remnants to Vishwaksen. Then, taking Vishwaksen's permission, he should himself honor the Lord's prasadam.

Vishwaksen is an associate of the Lord, but the worship of the Lord's devotees is formalized as part of worship of the Lord Himself. This is called *āvaraṇa-pūjā*. The *Hari-bhakti-vilāsa* says that one should offer Krishna's prasad to the Lord's devotees with the mantra *sarva-vaiṣṇavebhyo namaḥ* as a part of the process of puja. Gopala Bhatta Goswami there gives a mantra that lists a number of great devotees to whom one should make such an offering.

balir vibhīṣaṇo bhīṣmaḥ
kapilo nārado'rjunaḥ
prahlādaś cāmbarīṣaś ca
vasur vāyu-sutaḥ sivaḥ
viṣvaksenoddhavākrūraḥ
sanakādyāḥ śukādayaḥ
śrī-kṛṣṇasya prasādo'yaṁ
sarve gṛhṇantu vaiṣṇavāḥ

> May Bali, Vibhishana, Bhishma, Kapila, Narada, Arjuna, Prahlada, Ambarish, Vasu, Hanuman, Shiva, Vishwaksen, Uddhava, Akrura, the four Kumaras headed by Sanaka and the sages headed by Shukadeva accept these remnants of Lord Krishna. *HBV 8.215-6*

Thus Lord Gauranga was following perfectly the ritual process as described in the Agamas and the Bhagavatam: worshiping the Lord's eternal associates, the nitya siddha Vaishnavas, in His puja of Govinda. Without the mercy of those who are close to the Lord, we can never attain Him.

CHAPTER 3

Krishna's Mercy Comes Through *the* Devotees

Lord Shiva, the greatest of the Lord's devotees, once told his wife, Parvati Devi:

ārādhanānāṁ sarveṣāṁ
viṣṇor ārādhanaṁ param
tasmāt parataraṁ devi
tadīyānāṁ samarcanam

> Of all types of worship, worship of Lord Vishnu is best. Even better than the worship of Lord Vishnu, however, is the worship of those who are intimately connected to him (*tadīya*).
>
> *CC 2.11.31*

The Lord is under the control of those who have spotless love for Him. The Lord never accepts those who show disrespect for His devotees while making a show of devotion to Him. Krishna Himself said to Arjuna:

ye me bhakta-janāḥ pārtha
na me bhaktāś ca te janāḥ
mad-bhaktānāṁ ca ye bhaktās
te me bhaktatamā matāḥ

> O Arjuna, those who claim to be My devotees are actually not My devotees. I consider only those who are the servants of My devotees to factually be My devotees.
>
> *Ādi-purāṇa*

In His teachings to His beloved devotee Uddhava in the Srimad Bhagavatam, Lord Krishna lists those activities that He calls "the supreme causes of devotion" (*mad-bhakteḥ kāraṇaṁ param*):

bhakti-yogaḥ puraivoktaḥ
prīyamāṇāya te 'nagha
punaś ca kathayiṣyāmi
mad-bhakteḥ kāraṇaṁ param

> O sinless one! Out of affection for you, I previously described bhakti yoga in detail. Now I shall again recount the supreme causes of devotion to Me.
>
> *SB 11.19.19*

By "supreme causes of devotion," Krishna means the practices, or sadhana, that lead to bhakti; that is, the means by which one comes to experience the supreme devotion to the Lord (prema). These are:

śraddhāmṛta-kathāyāṁ me
śaśvan mad-anukīrtanam
pariniṣṭhā ca pūjāyāṁ
stutibhiḥ stavanaṁ mama

> Faith in hearing My nectarean topics; constant chanting of My name and pastimes; deep commitment to worshiping Me in the deity form, and praising Me with hymns and prayers; *SB 11.19.20*

ādaraḥ paricaryāyāṁ
sarvāṅgair abhivandanam
mad-bhakta-pūjābhyadhikā

sarva-bhūteṣu man-matiḥ

An affection for rendering service to Me; offering obeisances to Me through the use of all one's bodily limbs and faculties; considering the worship of other devotees to be even more important than My worship; being conscious of Me in all living beings; *SB 11.19.21*

The last line, *sarva-bhūteṣu man-matiḥ*, means "recognizing My presence in all living beings as the Supersoul." Srila Prabhupada Bhaktisiddhanta Saraswati notes here that one respects all living beings because they are in some way or another engaged in God's service.

Lord Krishna continues:

mad-artheṣv aṅga-ceṣṭā ca
vacasā mad-guṇeraṇam
mayy arpaṇaṁ ca manasaḥ
sarva-kāma-vivarjanam

Engaging all the bodily limbs to carry out My desires; using the power of speech to glorify My virtues; offering the activity of the mind to Me; giving up all material desires; *SB 11.19.22*

mad-arthe'rtha-parityāgo
bhogasya ca sukhasya ca
iṣṭaṁ dattaṁ hutaṁ japtaṁ
mad-arthaṁ yad vrataṁ tapaḥ

Renouncing all one's most valuable possessions for My sake, and dedicating the results of one's worship, charity, sacrifice, meditation, austerities or vows to Me. *SB 11.19.23*

He then concludes by saying,

evaṁ dharmair manuṣyāṇām
uddhavātma-nivedinām
mayi sañjāyate bhaktiḥ
ko'nyo'rtho 'syāvaśiṣyate

O Uddhava, by engaging in these activities, those who have surrendered themselves to Me experience the awakening of devotion to Me. And what else is left to be gained by one who has achieved love for Me? *SB 11.19.24*

From the above verses, Vrindavan Das selects the line *mad-bhakta-pūjābhyadhikā* and paraphrases it at the beginning of Chaitanya Bhagavata:

āmāra bhaktera pūjā āmā haite baṛa
sei prabhu vede bhāgavate kaila daṛha

The Lord has forcefully declared in the Vedas and the Bhagavatam: "Worshiping or serving My devotee is even greater than worshiping Me." *Cbh 1.1.8*

At the beginning of the above series of verses (11.19.19), Krishna says that He had "previously described bhakti yoga in detail." That summary of devotional activities in union with the Lord came earlier on in the Eleventh Canto, in the eleventh chapter, where the Lord answered Uddhava's question about how the sadhus spend their time. After describing the qualities of such a sadhu, culminating with the conclusion that the topmost devotees (*bhaktatama*) are those who in knowledge or in ignorance worship Him with single-minded devotion, the Lord lists their activities as follows:

mal-liṅga-mad-bhakta-jana-
darśana-sparśanārcanam
paricaryā stutiḥ prahva-
guṇa-karmānukīrtanam

O Uddhava! The saintly devotees are

engaged in looking at My image or at My devotees, in touching them, worshiping them, serving them, praising them and glorifying their wonderful qualities and deeds; *SB 11.11.34*

mat-kathā-śravaṇe śraddhā
mad-anudhyānam uddhava
sarva-lābhopaharaṇaṁ
dāsyenātma-nivedanam

They have faith in hearing about Me; they are constantly meditating on Me, making gifts to Me of everything that they earn or gain, and surrendering to Me in an attitude of service; *SB 11.11.35*

maj-janma-karma-kathanaṁ
mama parvānumodanam
gīta-tāṇḍava-vāditra-
goṣṭhībhir mad-gṛhotsavaḥ

They are always speaking of My appearance in this world and My other pastimes, observing the holy days and festive occasions connected to Me, and celebrating these festivals in My temple with songs, dance and music in the company of My devotees; *SB 11.11.36*

yātrā bali-vidhānaṁ ca
sarva-vārṣika-parvasu
vaidikī tāntrikī dīkṣā
madīya-vrata-dhāraṇam

They are always going on pilgrimage to My holy places and making special offerings on all the annual holy days; they take both Vedic and Pancharatrika initiation and observe fasts and other vows on Ekadasi; *SB 11.11.37*

mamārcā-sthāpane śraddhā
svataḥ saṁhatya codyamaḥ
udyānopavanākrīḍa-
pura-mandira-karmaṇi

They have faith in the rituals that consecrate My deity form in a temple and spontaneously work, either alone or with others, in growing gardens, orchards or parks around My temple; *SB 11.11.38*

sammārjanopalepābhyāṁ
seka-maṇḍala-vartanaiḥ
gṛha-śuśrūṣaṇaṁ mahyaṁ
dāsa-vad yad amāyayā

They are always sweeping the temple and washing it, sprinkling scented water in My temple, drawing auspicious designs with rice paste, and engaging in other kinds of service without false pride, only thinking of themselves as My servants; *SB 11.11.39*

amānitvam adambhitvaṁ
kṛtasyāparikīrtanam
api dīpāvalokaṁ me
nopayuñjyān niveditam

They are free from pride and hypocrisy, never boasting of the service they have done for Me, never using the lamp that has been lit in My temple for any other purpose; *SB 11.11.40*

yad yad iṣṭatamaṁ loke
yac cāti-priyam ātmanaḥ
tat tan nivedayen mahyaṁ
tad ānantyāya kalpate

And finally, they offer Me whatever is dearest to them. Offering Me what one loves oneself leads to infinite beatitude. *SB 11.11.41*

Anyone who truly loves the Lord will spontaneously engage in all these activities, which are in fact ways of serving the Lord. A devotee constantly engages in activities like chanting the Lord's names, hearing and discussing His pastimes, qualities, form and beauty.

Of all the limbs of devotional service, how-

THE SIMPLEST YET MOST EFFICACIOUS MEANS OF ACHIEVING KRISHNA'S MERCY... IS TO BECOME ATTACHED TO THE FELLOWSHIP OF HIS DEVOTEES.

ever, there is one that is the simplest yet most efficacious means of achieving Krishna's mercy, and that is to become attached to the fellowship of His devotees. Because Krishna subjects Himself to the love of His devotees, if we somehow come to love them and receive their merciful glance, then the Lord quickly makes us heirs to the treasure of ecstatic love that is so rare and difficult for others to attain. Therefore, the scriptures announce with the beating of drums and blowing of bugles that no one can attain pure devotion without the mercy of a devotee.

If, however, we neglect the company of pure devotees, all of our devotional activities are so much wasted effort, like offerings thrown on ashes rather than the sacrificial flame.

sādhu-saṅge kṛṣṇa-bhaktye śraddhā jadi haya
bhakti-phala prema haya saṁsāra jāya kṣaya
mahat-kṛpā vinā kona karme bhakti naya
kṛṣṇa-bhakti dūre rahu saṁsāra nahe kṣaya

Unless one is favored by a great devotee, no activity can be considered to possess the characteristics of devotional service. One cannot even be relieved from the bondage of material existence, what to speak of attaining love for Krishna.
CC 2.22.49,51

sādhu saṅga sādhu saṅga sarva śāstra kaya
lava-mātra sādhu saṅge sarva siddhi haya

All the scriptures glorify the association of devotees again and again. Just a moment's contact with the devotees results in all perfection. *CC 2.22.54*

Vrindavan Das writes in Chaitanya Bhagavata—

mora bhakta nā pūje āmāre pūje mātra
se dāmbhika nahe mora prasādera pātra

The Lord says, "If someone does not worship My devotee, prefering to worship Me alone, then I consider him a hypocrite and withhold My blessings from him." *Cbh 3.6.98*

The LORD SUBORDINATES HIMSELF *to His* DEVOTEE

Though the Lord is worshipable by all, He accepts the devotee as the object of His own devotion. He does not exist independently of His devotee. If the devotee awakens Him, He gets up; if the devotee gives Him a seat, He sits, and if the devotee feeds Him, He eats. The devotee is His heart and He is the heart of the devotee. The Lord knows nothing but His devotee, and the devotee knows nothing other than the Lord. The Lord calls none but the devotee His own; He finds the happiest home in the devotee's heart, for it has been made soft by the unrelenting desire to always render Him service.

The Lord loudly proclaimed this fact in the famous story of Ambarish (Ninth Canto, Srimad Bhagavatam). When Durvasa was unable to find refuge anywhere from the Sudarshan Chakra that pursued him, he went to see Lord Narayan. Narayan then glorified the devotees and expressed His love for them in terms that are unequalled anywhere in the scriptures. He said:

ahaṁ bhakta-parādhino
hy asvatantra iva dvija
sādhubhir grasta hṛdayo
bhaktair bhakta-jana-priyaḥ

"O Brahmin! I am completely under the control of My devotees. I have no freedom. My heart has been swallowed up by the saintly devotees, for I am their dear beloved. *SB 9.4.63*

nāham ātmānam āśāse
mad-bhaktaiḥ sādhubhir vinā
śriyaṁ cātyantikīṁ brahman
yeṣāṁ gatir ahaṁ parā

"I have no desire to enjoy My own transcendental bliss or My supreme opulences without the saintly devotees for whom I am the only goal in life. *SB 9.4.64*

ye dārāgāra-putrāpta-
prāṇān vittam imaṁ param

hitvā māṁ śaraṇaṁ yātāḥ
kathaṁ tāṁs tyaktum utsahe

"How could I possibly abandon those holy persons who for My sake have given up their homes, wives, children, relatives, possessions, even their lives and hopes for happiness in this world and the next? *SB 9.4.65*

mayi nirbaddha-hṛdayāḥ
sādhavaḥ sama-darśanāḥ
vaśīkurvanti māṁ bhaktyā
sat-striyaḥ sat-patiṁ ya

"A faithful wife wins her husband's love by her loyal devotion. I have similarly been won over by the saints who worship Me with attachment while treating all My creatures with equal affection. *SB 9.4.66*

mat-sevayā pratītaṁ te
sālokyādi-catuṣṭayam
necchanti sevayā pūrṇāḥ
kuto 'nyat kāla-viplutam

"My devotees are completely satisfied by their service to Me. As they await the opportunity to serve Me, they are not distracted by even the four kinds of liberation, which come to them anyway as a side effect of their service. Is it any wonder that they have no interest in lesser achievements like heaven, which are subject to the ravages of time? *SB 9.4.67*

sādhavo hṛdayaṁ mahyaṁ
sādhūnāṁ hṛdayaṁ tv aham
mad-anyat te na jānanti
nāhaṁ tebhyo manāg api

"I am the heart of the devotees and they

are My heart. They know nothing other than Me, and I know nothing other than them." *SB 9.4.68*

Thus Narottam Das Thakur sings—

bhaktera hṛdaye govindera satata viśrāma
govinda kahena mama bhakta se parāṇa

Govinda always takes rest in the heart of His devotee. He says, "My devotees are My entire life." *Prārthanā*

The devotee is all in all to Krishna, and Krishna is all in all to the devotee. Neither the devotee nor Krishna can tolerate even a moment's separation from each other. It is clear, then, that anyone who wishes to attain Krishna's mercy must first seek the intercession of His devotee. Bhaktivinode Thakur shows how this is to be done in the following prayer from *Kalyāṇa-kalpa-taru*—

kabe śrī caitanya more karibena dayā
kabe āmi paiba vaiṣṇava-pada-chāyā

Oh when will Sri Chaitanya Mahaprabhu bestow His mercy upon me? When will I find shelter in the shade of a Vaishnava's lotus feet?

kabe āmi chāḍiba e viśayābhimāna
kabe viṣṇu-jane āmi koriba sammāna

When will I renounce pride in my possessions and properly honor those who have dedicated themselves to Lord Vishnu?

gala-vastra kṛtāñjali vaiṣṇava-nikaṭe
dante tṛṇa kari' dāṅḍāibo niṣkapaṭe

In a very humble, submissive mood and without duplicity, I will stand before the Vaishnavas with my cloth wrapped around my neck, my hands folded and a blade of grass between my teeth.

kāṅdiyā kāṅdiyā janāiba duḥkha-grāma
saṁsāra-anala haite māgiba viśrāma

With tears streaming down my cheeks, I will tell the Vaishnava of all the miseries I have undergone and beg for relief from the blazing fire of material life.

śuniyā āmāra duḥkha vaiṣṇava ṭhākura
āmā lāgi' kṛṣṇa āvedibena pracura

When the venerable Vaishnava hears of my sufferings, he will sincerely petition the Lord on my behalf.

vaiṣṇavera āvedane kṛṣṇa dayāmaya
e hena pāmara prati ha'bena sadaya

In response to his prayer, the all-merciful Lord Krishna will then display His compassion towards me, sinful though I am.

vinodera nivedana vaiṣṇava-caraṇe
kṛpā kari' saṅge laha ei akiñcane

Bhaktivinode prays to the lotus feet of the Vaishnavas, "Please mercifully give your shelter and association to this destitute person."
(Kalyāṇa-kalpa-taru, Dainyamayī prārthanā, 1)

It is only through the medium of the Vaishnava that we can attain the mercy of the Lord.

Chapter 4

Association *is* *the* Root *of* Devotion

The scriptures describe the steps that lead from the first planting of the seed of devotion up to its flowering in pure love of God. All the scriptures agree, however, that the devotional life begins and ends with sadhu sanga. Lord Chaitanya Mahaprabhu gave the following instruction to Sanatan Goswami:

kṛṣṇa bhakti janma mūla haya sādhu saṅga
kṛṣṇa prema janme tiṅho punaḥ mukhya aṅga

> The root cause of devotional service to Lord Krishna is contact with advanced devotees. Yet even after one's dormant love for Krishna has awakened, the companionship of such devotees remains the chief element in one's devotional life. CC 2.22.80

Devotional service can only come about when one has been blessed by a pure devotee of Krishna.

Bhaktivinode Thakur paraphrases this verse in his *Amṛta-pravāha-bhāṣya* commentary, "Though association with devotees presents itself at the very beginning of the devotional path and is indeed the root cause of one's taking up the devotional life, it nevertheless continues to be considered one of the primary limbs of devotional service even after one has attained the highest summit of devotional perfection."

There is thus an unbreakable relationship between devotional service and association with devotees. Anyone who wishes to perfect the life of devotion cannot afford to neglect keeping company with devotees.

mahat-kṛpā vinā kono karme bhakti naya
kṛṣṇa-bhakti dūre rahu saṁsāra nahe kṣaya

> Unless one receives the blessings of a great devotee, no activity qualifies as devotion. Not only is one unable to attain devotion to Krishna, one cannot even be freed from the bondage of material existence. CC 2.22.51

Srila Bhaktisiddhanta Saraswati Prabhupada has commented on the above couplet in his *Anubhāṣya* as follows: "No amount of ritual activity in the Karma Kanda section of the Vedas can produce transcendental devotional service to Krishna. Devotional service can only come about when one has been blessed by a pure devotee of Krishna. However, it is not simply devotional service that remains outside the purview of the person who has been deprived of such blessings—one cannot even count on overcoming the material conceptions that keep one bound within the entanglements of mundane life. No real greatness can possibly manifest in a living entity who is void of devotion to Krishna, for only a devotee of Krishna is truly transcendental to the material energy. According to purely material considerations, one may find it impossible to understand how this is so and continue to think the devotee is as materially bound as the next person, but the truth is that he has abandoned all things mundane and has attached himself to the Lord, the supreme, transcendental goal of life. As such, should one recognize the pure devotee, know him to be the true well-wisher of all living beings and beg sincerely for his mercy, one will be unburdened of the desire to enjoy this material world. He will be freed from its sufferings and become eligible to engage in pure devotional service to the Lord."

In the Fifth Canto of the Srimad Bhagavatam, the great devotee Bharata clearly shows that apart from the blessings of a devotee, there is no other means for attaining devotion to Krishna. In his homily to Rahugana, the king of Sindhu Sauvira, he says—

rahūgaṇaitat tapasā na yāti
na cejyayā nirvapaṇād gṛhād vā
na cchandasā naiva jalāgni-sūryair
vinā mahat-pāda-rajo-bhiṣekam

> O Rahugana, one cannot realize the Absolute Truth unless one smears his entire body with the dust of the lotus feet of great devotees. Such realization cannot come from penances and austerities, nor from performing sacrifice, renunciation of family life, nor from learning, nor by undergoing severe penances such as keeping oneself submerged in water in winter or surrounding oneself by fire and the scorching heat of the sun in summer. *SB 5.12.12*

In other words, without the blessings of a great devotee, the perfect execution of our regulative duties in Varnashram Dharma will not bring us pure knowledge of God, nor result in pure devotion to Him.

The child devotee Prahlada similarly glorifies the dust of the Vaishnavas' feet to his evil father, Hiranyakashipu—

naiṣāṁ matis tāvad urukramāṅghriṁ
spṛśaty anarthāpagamo yad arthaḥ
mahīyasāṁ pāda-rajo'bhiṣekaṁ
niṣkiñcanānāṁ na vṛṇīta yāvat

> As long as people do not powder themselves with the dust of the lotus feet of a completely selfless Vaishnava, they will never be able to approach the glorious Lord, who alone can drive away all undesirable things from their hearts. *SB 7.5.32*

The Lord is the *artha*, the meaning or value that destroys all the anarthas, those meaningless, valueless or undesirable things that clutter and confuse our lives.

Both Bharata and Prahlada's verses use the words *pāda-rajo'bhiṣeka*. The *abhiṣeka* is literally the ritual bath that consecrated a king as the legitimate ruler of a country, or a guru as his spiritual master's legitimate successor. Thus the receipt of the Vaishnava's blessings is compared to a sanctifying bath that radically transforms a person's status from non-devotee to devotee. Only through the blessings of the devotee can one be freed from the undesirable things in one's heart and thus attain Krishna's lotus feet.

The KEY *is* COMMITMENT

In chapter twenty two of the Chaitanya Charitamrita's Madhya Lila, Krishna Das Kaviraj Goswami describes the sixty-four limbs of devotional service, but specifies that of these, five are superior to all the rest:

sādhu-saṅga nāma-kīrtana
bhāgavata-śravaṇa
mathurā-vāsa śrī-mūrtira
śraddhāya sevana

> Associating with devotees, chanting the Holy Names of the Lord, hearing the Srimad Bhagavatam, residing in Mathura and worshiping the Lord's deity form with faith and veneration. *CC 2.22.124*

sakala-sādhana-śreṣṭha ei pañca aṅga
kṛṣṇa-prema janmāya ei pāñcera alpa saṅga

eka aṅga sādhe keha sādhe bahu aṅga
niṣṭhā haile upajaya premera taraṅga

These five limbs of devotional service are the best of all. Even the slight performance of any one of them awakens love for Krishna. Whether a person executes only one of these processes of devotional service or all of them, the waves of love of Godhead will well up as a result of his commitment to the practice, or nishtha. *CC 2.22.125, 129*

The key word here is nishtha, or commitment. Unless one commits oneself fully to at least one of these devotional practices, there is no possibility that it will bear fruit and award the aspirant with love for Krishna. Srila Bhaktisiddhanta Saraswati comments, "As a result of engaging in devotional practices, one's undesirable proclivities are removed and one becomes committed to Krishna and service to Him. This commitment eventually leads one to prema, or love for God."

CC 2.22.129, Anubhāṣya

The symptom of one who has reached the stage of commitment to the devotional path or nishtha is *avikṣepeṇa sātatyam*—constancy in one's practice through freedom from all external and internal distractions.

In the First Canto, second chapter of the Srimad Bhagavatam, Suta Goswami addresses Shaunaka Rishi and the sixty thousand sages assembled at Naimisharanya, saying that the person who has accumulated the type of pious acts that lead to devotion develops a taste for hearing Krishna katha from the mouths of his spiritual master and the Vaishnavas. As this taste grows, he remains constantly rapt in meditation on these matters. This constant meditation on Krishna is like a sword that cuts through the ropes of karma that bind him, through all the results of prior actions that were to have been suffered or enjoyed in this or future lifetimes. Who then in this world would not find hearing about Krishna worthwhile?

yad-anudhyāsinā yuktāḥ
karma-granthi-nibandhanam
chindanti kovidās tasya
ko na kuryāt kathā-ratim

Equipped with the sword of constant meditation on Krishna, the intelligent cut through the ropes of karma that bind them. Who then will not take pleasure in hearing about Krishna, which makes such meditation possible?

SB 1.2.15

In their ignorance, the conditioned souls are absorbed in their bodily and mental designations and bewildered by false ego. They engage in rituals, austerities and other religious activities, but unless they purify the consciousness, these things only increase their material bondage rather than put an end to it. The taste for hearing about Krishna that comes from associating with a great devotee, or mahat, cuts right through this bondage.

In the Bhagavad Gita, Krishna explains the true meaning of sacrifice:

yajñārthāt karmaṇo'nyatra
loko'yaṁ karma-bandhanaḥ
tad-arthaṁ karma kaunteya
mukta-saṅgaḥ samācara

This world is a source of bondage when work is not performed as a sacrifice to Vishnu. Therefore, O son of Kunti, do everything for His sake, free from any selfish intent. *Gita 3.9*

The word *yajña* (sacrifice) means any activity that is done as an offering to the Supreme Lord without any desire for oneself. In this verse, it is said that any work not done in this spirit results in bondage. Even works that are done on behalf of the Supreme Lord Vishnu result in bondage if one performs them with the hope of enjoying the fruits. Therefore Krishna warns us to perform such sacrificial acts free from any such intent—*mukta-saṅgaḥ samācara*. Srila Bhaktivinode Thakur comments, "Even ordinary activities carried out in this consciousness lead to the practice of devotion and, through that, to an understanding of God's nature. In this way, one gradually obtains devotion beyond the modes of material nature."

Chance Encounter *with the* Vaishnavas

After glorifying the benefits of hearing Hari katha, Suta Goswami continues his discourse by telling how the taste for hearing such topics develops—

śuśrūṣoḥ śraddadhānasya
vāsudeva-kathā-ruciḥ
syān mahat-sevayā viprāḥ
puṇya-tīrtha-niṣevaṇāt

O sages, for a person with faith in the scriptures and a service mentality, the taste for hearing about Lord Krishna comes about through serving a great Vaishnava and by visiting the holy places of pilgrimage. *SB 1.2.16*

Vishwanath Chakravarti Thakur comments on this verse as follows: "The words *mahat-sevayā* found in this verse refer to the chance encounter with a great Vaishnava. One who subsequently renders service to him develops faith in his words. The word *puṇya-tīrtha-niṣevaṇāt* should thus be interpreted as taking shelter of a spiritual master, rather than simply visiting places of pilgrimage. When we have taken shelter and are eager to hear, we develop a taste for the topics of Lord Krishna." [2]

Srila Bhaktisiddhanta Saraswati Thakur also comments on this verse in his *Vivṛti*: "It is here stated that those who wish to find pleasure in hearing Hari katha should render service to two objects. The pure devotee's heart is a holy place, but the place where such a devotee resides is also transformed into a holy place of pilgrimage—indeed, it is said that it is equal to all the holy places. So both the devotee and the holy place where he resides are designated by the term *puṇya-tīrtha*. Both of these holy places enkindle one's desire to hear about Krishna. More than the tirtha, or place itself, however, direct service to a great Vaishnava awakens this taste for hearing about Krishna. The Bhagavata says that all good qualities take up residence in a devotee who is engaged selflessly in the service of the Lord (*yasyāsti bhaktir bhagavaty akiñcanā*, SB 5.18.12). A person who is detached from everything except Krishna and is endowed with all the virtues is known as a great soul or mahat."

The taste for hearing about Krishna that comes from associating with a great devotee, or mahat, cuts right through this bondage.

In the Tenth Canto, Akrura offers his prayers to Krishna in the following two verses:

notsahe'haṁ kṛpaṇa-dhīḥ
kāma-karma-hataṁ manaḥ
roddhuṁ pramāthibhiś cākṣair
hriyamāṇam itas tataḥ

"My intelligence is so miserly that I am unable to overcome my mind, which is constantly agitated by desires and the effects of my desires, being pulled this way and that by the powerful senses. *SB 10.40.27*

so'haṁ tavāṅghry-upagato'smy asatāṁ durāpaṁ
tac cāpy ahaṁ bhavad-anugraha īśa manye
puṁso bhaved yarhi saṁsaraṇāpavargas
tvayy abja-nābha sad-upāsanayā matiḥ syāt

"O lotus-navelled Lord! If a person such as I has still been able to approach Your lotus feet, which are unattainable by the commonplace, it is the result of Your mercy alone. It is only when the time comes for one's material entanglement to end that one is able to meet and serve a saintly person through whom the propensity to serve You is imbibed." SB 10.40.28

If we look carefully at the wording of this verse, we will see that Akrura's intention is to say that one comes to God only through the blessings of a saintly devotee. Vishwanath Chakravarti states this clearly in his commentary:

> If Krishna should ask when one attains His blessings, Akrura answers, "O lotus-navelled Lord! When the propensity to serve You has been imbibed through meeting and serving a saintly person." And when will such service take place? "When the time comes for one to be liberated from one's material entanglement. That is, when the time comes for it to end." And when does the time come for one's material entanglement to end? "When some great saint spontaneously or causelessly gives his blessing." This verse thus describes the sequence of events in attaining liberation: One first fortuitously receives the blessings of a saint and from that moment his entanglement in material life starts to undergo the process by which it will be destroyed. As a part of this process, the devotee begins living in the company of the saintly and serving them. This then results in his becoming attached to Krishna.[3]

For a person with faith in the scriptures and a service mentality, the taste for hearing about Lord Krishna comes about through serving a great Vaishnava and by visiting the holy places of pilgrimage.

King Muchukunda similarly states in his prayers to Krishna that when "the time" comes, a fortuitous encounter with a saintly devotee takes place:

bhavāpavargo bhramato yadā bhavej
janasya tarhy acyuta sat-samāgamaḥ
sat-saṅgamo yarhi tadaiva sad-gatau
parāvareśe tvayi jāyate ratiḥ

> O infallible Lord! When the time has come for someone wandering throughout the universes to be finished with his material existence, he comes into contact with a devotee. Only as a result of such associaton with devotees can anyone develop an attraction for You, the Lord of the universe and ultimate destination of the saintly. SB 10.51.53

Vishwanath Chakravarti cites Sanatan Goswami's *Vaiṣṇava-toṣaṇī* in explaining this verse:

> Krishna might ask Muchukunda the question, "Without My blessings, no one can come into contact with a true saint. So are My blessings not the ultimate and original cause of one's being liberated?" In response, Muchukunda says, "Krishna, You place all Your hopes in Your devotees, just as You are their only refuge. Therefore, though Lord Brahma correctly (10.14.2) said that You are completely independent (*svecchāmaya*), it was explained in that context that this means You do everything in accordance with the desire of Your devotees, for You once told Durvasa (9.4.67) that You are completely dependent on them." Since the Lord is controlled by His devotees' love, everything He does is really done on their behalf and in accordance with their desires. The conclusion is thus that whatever blessings the Lord bestows come as a result of the blessings given by His devotees.[4]

The Lord is the supreme refuge of the devotee. Indeed, He is the ultimate refuge of everything in the universe. Nevertheless, He seeks refuge in the heart of His devotee. Narottam das Thakur has expressed this nicely—

bhaktera hṛdaye govindera satata viśrāma
govinda kahena mama bhakta se parāṇa

The Vaishnava's heart is Lord Govinda's eternal resting place. He says, "My devotees are My life." *Prārthanā*

The Supreme Lord is completely independent, but when it comes to His devotee, He is ready to give up this independence for His devotee's sake. The devotee is the Lord's one and only treasure, the life of His life. Thus if anyone wishes to attain the mercy of the Lord, he must first do everything he can to attain the mercy of the Lord's devotee—become the servant of the servant. The Lord Himself states *mat-pūjābhyadhikā*, "worship of My devotee is greater than even My worship." He says, "My devotees have swallowed up My heart. They are My heart and I am theirs. They know nothing other than Me, and I nothing other than them." Therefore, it is rightly said that just a moment's association with the devotees results in all perfection.

Knowing that one's advancement in devotional life depends on the mercy of the devotees at every step, Srila Bhaktivinode Thakur prays to Lord Chaitanya Mahaprabhu for "a place in the shade of a Vaishnava's lotus feet." One should take a humble posture—wrapping one's cloth around the neck and standing with folded hands—and sincerely beg the devotee to cleanse the heart of any desire that leads us away from Krishna. If the devotee intercedes with Krishna on our behalf, telling Him of our miserable situation, then Krishna will surely respond. Bhaktivinode Thakur concludes—

vaiṣṇavera āvedane kṛṣṇa dayāmaya
e heno pāmara prati ha'bena sadaya

In response to the Vaishnava's prayer, the all-merciful Sri Krishna will then display His compassion towards even the most wicked person. *Kalyāṇa-kalpa-taru*

This, then, is the best means of attaining the Lord's mercy.

bhakta-pada-dhūli āra bhakta-pada-jala
bhakta-bhukta-avaśeṣa tina mahā-bala
ei tina-sevā haite kṛṣṇa-premā haya
punaḥ punaḥ sarva-śāstre phukāriyā kaya

The dust of a devotee's feet, the water that has washed his feet, and the remnants of his food are three very powerful aids to spiritual practice. All revealed scriptures loudly declare again and again that one can attain the supreme goal of ecstatic love for Krishna through the use of these three substances. *CC 3.16.60-61*

The PROCESS *of* PURIFICATION ACCORDING *to* SUTA GOSWAMI

Let us return to Suta Goswami's introductory comments at the beginning of his recital, where he describes the effects of hearing Krishna-centered literature like the Srimad Bhagavatam—

śṛṇvatāṁ sva-kathāḥ kṛṣṇaḥ
puṇya-śravaṇa-kīrtanaḥ
hṛdy antaḥstho hy abhadrāṇi
vidhunoti suhṛt-satām

Hearing about Krishna and glorifying Him is a most holy activity, for when the aspiring devotee listens to such topics, Krishna, who resides in his heart, destroys all the inauspiciousness that still remains there. *SB 1.2.17*

In this verse, the words *puṇya-śravaṇa-kīrtanaḥ* are an epithet of Krishna meaning that hearing about Him and glorifying Him are most pious activities. Krishna is the well-wisher of the pious and He is the indwelling spiritual master, or *caittya-guru*. As such, when we devotedly listen to His names, qualities and pastimes from a pure devotee, then the indwelling Lord will remove from our hearts all the inauspicious desires for sense gratification, liberation and mystic power—everything that is detrimental to advancement on the devotional path.

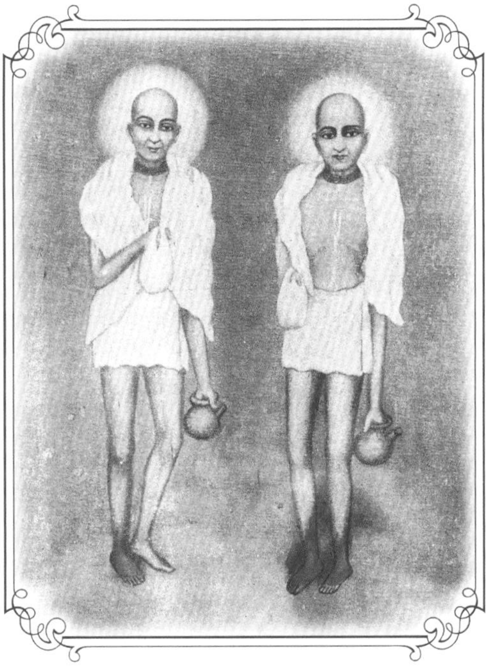

By constantly serving the devotee Bhagavata and hearing the Srimad Bhagavatam from him, all our sinful reactions will come to the point where they are almost completely eradicated. The devotees attain a fixed, unshakeable devotion to the Supreme Lord in His playful manifestation as the Lila Purushottam, Sri Krishna. In this state, they are no longer subject to distractions.

naṣṭa-prāyeṣv abhadreṣu
nityaṁ bhāgavata-sevayā
bhagavaty uttama-śloke
bhaktir bhavati naiṣṭhikī

When all of one's sins are practically destroyed through constant hearing of the Srimad Bhagavatam and serving the devotees, then one comes to the stage of steadfast devotion to the Supreme Lord, who is glorified in the choicest verses.

SB 1.2.18

With the removal of all these anarthas—the lust, greed, anger, bewilderment, intoxication and envy that arise from the modes of passion and ignorance, and which disrupt the practice of devotion—no obstacles remain to prevent the mind from being fixed in pure goodness. In this state, the practitioner feels peace and happiness.

tadā rajas-tamo-bhāvāḥ
kāma-lobhādayaś ca ye
ceta etair anābiddhaṁ
sthitaṁ sattve prasīdati

At this point, the lust, desire and hankering that are produced by the material nature's modes of passion and ignorance no longer disrupt the devotee's consciousness. Thus established in goodness, he feels perfectly contented. *SB 1.2.19*

In this way, one attains peace of mind through the practice of bhakti yoga. Then it becomes possible to see the Lord.

evaṁ prasanna-manaso
bhagavad-bhakti-yogataḥ
bhagavat-tattva-vijñānaṁ
mukta-saṅgasya jāyate

Thus peaceful in mind through the practice of devotional service, one is liberated from all attachments and attains full realization of the nature of the Supreme Lord. *SB 1.2.20*

Srila Jiva Goswami states that the words *bhagavat-tattva-vijñānaṁ* ("full realization of the nature of the Supreme Lord") means the complete experience of the Lord, up to and including a direct vision of the Lord's form. This, then, is the supreme achievement of spiritual life, and it begins with the association of pure devotees.

When we achieve full knowledge of the nature of the Supreme Lord as the all-pervading, indwelling Supersoul, we are freed from the bonds that tie the heart. In other words, the last strands of false ego that bind us to this world are severed, along with doubts about these divine truths. Finally, the entanglements that come from desires, acting on those desires and the consequences of such actions, are all completely destroyed.

bhidyate hṛdaya-granthiś
chidyante sarva-saṁśayāḥ
kṣīyante cāsya karmāṇi
dṛṣṭa evātmanīśvare

When one sees that the Supreme Lord is present within oneself, the knots in his heart are severed, all his doubts are removed, and all the consequences of his past deeds, pious or impious, are eradicated. *SB 1.2.21*[5]

The sequence of verses quoted above from Suta Goswami's introductory discourse to the Srimad Bhagavatam outlines the progressive path of devotional service. In his commentary to the last of these, Vishwanath Chakravarti summarizes the entire discussion with a pair of verses of his own composition that list a total of fourteen steps in all, from beginning to end:

satāṁ kṛpā mahat-sevā
śraddhā guru-padāśrayaḥ
bhajaneṣu spṛhā bhaktir
anarthāpagamas tataḥ

niṣṭhā rucir athāsaktī ratiḥ
premātha darśanam
harer mādhuryānubhava ity
arthāḥ syuś caturdaśe

(1) One first receives the blessings of a devotee; (2) one then engages in service to such a great soul (*mahat-sevā*); (3) one develops faith; (4) one takes shelter of a spiritual master in initiation; (5) one begins trying to perfect the performance of devotional practices; (6) one starts to experience devotion; and (7) one's anarthas begin to disappear. Next one proceeds through the stages of (8) steadfastness in devotional practice (nishtha), (9) taste (ruchi), (10) attachment (asakti), and (11) bhava. Then one comes to (12) the stage of ecstatic love (prema), followed by (13) the direct vision of the Lord, and (14) a full experience of the Lord's sweetness.

Other Descriptions *of the* Progressive Path

Gaudiya Vaishnavas will already be familiar with the summary of the progressive path of devotion found in the Chaitanya Charitamrita, which consists of nine stages. In this list, all the steps from faith up to to the seventh, attachment, fall within the category of abhidheya tattva. Bhava bhakti, the eighth stage, and prema, the ninth stage and ultimate goal, are considered to be the prayojan tattva, or state of perfection.

kono bhāgye kono jīvera śraddhā jadi haya
tabe sei jīva sādhu-saṅga je karaya
sādhu-saṅga haite haya śravaṇa-kīrtana
sādhana-bhaktye haya
sarvānartha-nivartana
anartha-nivṛtti haile bhaktye niṣṭhā haya
niṣṭhā haite śravaṇādye ruci upajaya
ruci haite bhaktye haya āsakti pracura
āsakti haite citte janme kṛṣṇe prīty-aṅkura
sei bhāva gāḍha haile dhare prema-nāma
sei premā prayojana sarvānanda-dhāma

If by some great good fortune, a certain living entity develops faith in Krishna, he begins to associate with devotees. As a result of associating with devotees, he takes up practical devotional service beginning with hearing and chanting. Such practical devotional service frees him from all unwanted material contamination and that leads to constancy. When one has nishtha or firmness in one's practice, then a taste for hearing and chanting and other practices arises. The next step is the awakening of a deep attachment, and from that attachment the first manifestations of love finally

> appear in the heart like a tree's seedling. These first ecstatic manifestations are called bhava, which intensify to become love of God, or prema, the ultimate goal of life and the reservoir of all pleasure.
> *CC 2.23.9-13*

This description is derived from the *Bhakti-rasāmṛta-sindhu,* where Rupa Goswami presents it in the following words—

ādau śraddhā tataḥ sādhu-
saṅgo'tha bhajana-kriyā
tato'nartha-nivṛttiḥ syāt
tato niṣṭhā rucis tataḥ
tathāsaktis tato bhāvas
tataḥ premābhyudañcati
sādhakānām ayaṁ premṇaḥ
prādurbhāve bhavet kramaḥ

> The progressive development of prema goes through faith, association with the saintly, the performance of devotional practices, the dissipation of contamination in the consciousness, firm commitment, taste, attachment, feeling and then love.
> *BRS 1.4.14-15*

The most abbreviated description of the progressive path is found in the Srimad Bhagavatam where Kapila Deva says to his mother Devahuti—

satāṁ prasaṅgān mama vīrya-saṁvido
bhavanti hṛt-karṇa-rasāyanāḥ kathāḥ
taj-joṣaṇād āśv apavarga-vartmani
śraddhā ratir bhaktir anukramiṣyati

> My heroic pastimes are very pleasing to the ear and satisfying to the heart when heard in the association of pure devotees. As a result of joyfully relishing these pastimes in such association, one quickly advances on the path of liberation, passing through the stages of faith (sraddha), the revelation of one's divine relationship with Krishna (rati), and true love for Him (bhakti). *SB 3.25.25*

In this verse, the word sraddha, or faith, includes the first seven stages of devotional advancement, which Rupa Goswami calls sadhana bhakti, or devotional service in practice. Rati is equivalent to bhava bhakti, while the word bhakti here means prema, or love for Krishna.

Thus, through hearing about Krishna from devotees, one develops faith in Krishna. Faith is the only qualification for the practice of devotion—*śraddhāvān jana haya bhakti-adhikārī.* Devotion arises through the association of devotees—*bhaktis tu bhagavad-bhakta-saṅgena parijāyate.* This is why Krishna Das Kaviraj has said that the association of devotees is the root of devotional service. He also says that one who has faith continues to associate with devotees. The meaning of this second association means taking shelter of a spiritual master and being initiated.

kono bhāgye kāro
saṁsāra kṣayonmukha haya
sādhu saṅge tare kṛṣṇe rati upajaya

> When, through good fortune, one's material condition is ripe for destruction, then through the association of devotees, he is liberated and his relation with Krishna is awakened. *CC 2.22.45*

sādhu-saṅge kṛṣṇa-bhaktye
śraddhā jadi haya
bhakti-phala prema haya,
saṁsāra jāya kṣaya

> If, through the association of the saintly, one develops faith in devotion to Krishna, then he will get the fruit of bhakti, love for Krishna, and his material entanglements will come to an end.
> *CC 2.22.49*

The word *bhāgya* or "good fortune" used here means "pious deeds" (*sukṛti*). There are three kinds of sukriti—the good deeds that lead to sense pleasure, other good deeds that lead to liberation, and those that lead to devotion. Activities that lead to devotion are called *bhakty-unmukhī sukṛti*; those that facilitate or lead to improved sense gratification are called *bhogonmukhī sukṛti*, and those that lead to liberation are called *mokṣonmukhī sukṛti*. Bhaktivinode Thakur writes in his *Amṛta-pravāha-bhāṣya* to Chaitanya Charitamrita 2.22.45, "When the pious deeds that lead to the destruction of one's material condition of life and the awakening of one's constitutional function of devotion to Krishna are about to bear fruit, one comes into the association of saintly devotees. Through this association one is liberated from the material condition and one's affection for Krishna is awakened."

The Devotional Creeper

When discussing Mahaprabhu's teachings to Rupa Goswami, we find the following information: According to their karma, the living entities take birth in different species of life within the fourteen planes of material existence. Of this infinite number of living beings, some fortunate individuals who have obtained the piety that comes out of devotional association are blessed with the mercy of the spiritual master and Krishna. This means that through Krishna's mercy one gets the blessings of a spiritual master and through the mercy of the spiritual master one attains the blessings of Krishna. Through these combined blessings, one is given faith, the seed for the creeper of devotion. One plants this seed in the heart and then waters it with the acts of hearing and chanting about Krishna, with the result that the seed sprouts and grows into a creeper or vine-like plant.

It is the nature of a creeper to search for a tree to support its growth, but in this material world there is no support for the creeper of devotion. Searching for its ultimate shelter, the creeper of devotion goes beyond the phenomenal world to a place known as the Viraja River, where the three modes of material nature are in perfect balance. Though this state of being is highly purifying, the creeper of devotional service still finds no support there.

Being watered by the processes of hearing and chanting, the creeper continues to flourish and grow, going beyond the realm of Brahma to attain the spiritual sky. Brahmaloka and the Viraja River are the dividing line between the material and spiritual worlds. The material world is also sometimes called the "realm of the Goddess," since it is under the dominance of Nature. The spiritual sky, where the qualities of material nature have no power, is also known as Vaikuntha. Nevertheless, only two and a half of the five kinds of relationships with the Supreme Lord are experienced by devotees of Narayan, who is the Lord of Vaikuntha. These are the moods of peace, i.e., inactive awe and reverence, servitorship and friendship. Since friendship with Narayan lacks intimacy, it is considered to be only a half-relationship. The other primary relationships (intimate friendship, protectiveness, and conjugal love) and the seven secondary relationships are manifest fully in Vrindavan, where Krishna is the central object of love.

Through Krishna's mercy one gets the blessings of a spiritual master and through the mercy of the spiritual master one attains the blessings of Krishna.

When the creeper of devotion finally reaches Vrindavan, it wraps itself around Lord Krishna's feet, which are like the wish-fulfilling tree that bears any fruit one could possibly desire. The creeper also begins to bear fruit—the ripe, juicy fruits of love for God. Before it can reach this ultimate shelter, however, there are thousands of obstacles that must be overcome, and the only means to do so is through fellowship with saintly devotees.

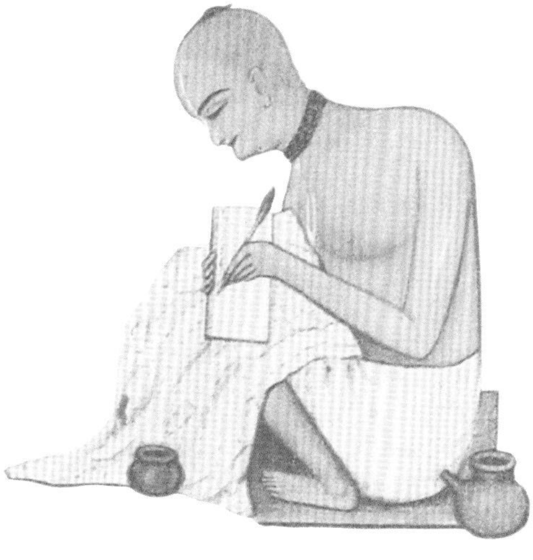

Chapter 5

Sadhu Sanga Must Accompany All Devotional Practices

The five principal devotional activities have been previously cited in a passage from Chaitanya Charitamrita. Of these, the fellowship of devotees, or sadhu sanga, has been singled out as the most important, for without such fellowship, the chanting of the Holy Name, discussing the Srimad Bhagavatam, or any other devotional activity is impossible. Krishna Das Kaviraj quotes several verses from the *Bhakti-rasāmṛta-sindhu*, on which he has based his own summary of the subject—

sajātīyāśaye snigdhe
sādhau saṅgaḥ svato vare
śrīmad-bhāgavatārthānām
āsvādo rasikaiḥ saha
śraddhā-viśeṣataḥ prītiḥ
śrī-mūrter aṅghri-sevane
nāma-saṅkīrtanaṁ śrīman-
mathurā-maṇḍale sthitiḥ
aṅgānāṁ pañcakasyāsya
pūrvaṁ vilikhitasya ca
nikhila-śraiṣṭhya-bodhāya
punar apy atra kīrtanam

Keeping the company of saintly persons who share the same spiritual mood, who are affectionate and more advanced than oneself; chanting the names of the Lord; residing in the region of Mathura; a love for serving the Lord in His deity form according to a special kind of faith; and relishing the topics of the Srimad Bhagavatam in the association of rasika devotees. Though these five pillars of devotion were mentioned previously, they have been repeated here in order to emphasize their centrality to the entire devotional process. *BRS 1.2.90-92*[6]

After naming these five as the best of all devotional processes, Srila Rupa Goswami goes on to say—

durūhādbhuta-vīrye'smin
śraddhā dūre'stu pañcake
yatra svalpo'pi sambandhaḥ
sad-dhiyāṁ bhāva-janmane

The amazing spiritual power of these five practices is difficult to comprehend. Even the smallest engagement in any one of them results in the awakening of divine ecstasy, even in the faithless, as long as they are pure-hearted. So we can just imagine their effectiveness for those who practice them with deep faith.
BRS 1.2.238

Jiva Goswami explains the word "pure-hearted" (*sad-dhiyām*) as meaning "untouched by offenses" (*niraparādha-cittānām*).

The adjectives used to describe these five devotional activities are *durūha* ("difficult to understand") and *adbhuta-vīrya* ("possessed of amazing power"). Though these adjectives apply equally to all five activities, they are especially applicable to the association of devotees, which must be given a place of honor among them. For it is said, *bhaktis tu bhagavad-bhakta-saṅgena parijāyate*—"Devotion arises out of association with devotees of the Lord." One first begins on the path of devotion when one hears the powerful subjects related to Krishna from the mouth of a pure devotee. Such devotion goes through the stages of practice, to the awakening of a personal relationship (*bhāva-bhakti*) and then to ecstatic love, as we have already seen stated by Kapila Deva to his mother Devahuti. *SB 3.25.25*

Sadhu sanga is the beginning and the end of devotional service, the essential element in all devotional activities, and a principal ingredient of success in spiritual life.

Srila Bhaktisiddhanta Saraswati's Commentary *on* Sadhu Sanga

In his *Anubhāṣya* (2.22.126-127), Srila Prabhupada Bhaktisiddhanta Saraswati has given a word-by-word analysis of the first two verses quoted above.

One should seek the fellowship of devotees who are here described as having three attributes: (1) *sajātīyāśaye* means that they should have the same inner desires, i.e., share the same devotional mood; (2) *snigdhe*, they should be deeply worthy of one's trust and confidence; and (3) they should, as far as possible, be more advanced than oneself.

One must seek out the association of devotees who have the same heartfelt desires: in other words, the desire to attain pure loving devotion for Radha Krishna according to the directions given by Sri Chaitanya Mahaprabhu. Such devotees will have a welcoming and affectionate attitude to one who seeks their association, as well as deep faith in the spiritual master, Chaitanya Mahaprabhu, and the Divine Couple Gandharvika and Giridhari. A relationship of faith and trust exists in the association of devotees, otherwise how can discussions of transcendental topics take place?

At the beginning of the Bhagavata, Shaunaka

also uses the word *snigdha* when he asks Suta to answer his questions without any reticence:

brūyuḥ snigdhasya śiṣyasya
guravo guhyam apy uta

> Teachers are obliged to reveal even the most confidential truths to their affectionate disciples. *SB 1.1.8*

Here, Sridhar Swami translates *snigdha* as "loving." Vishwanath Chakravarti Thakur elaborates on this, saying *guru-viṣayaka-premavataḥ*, "loving towards the teacher." A wise spiritual master with much experience in the practice of bhajan may thus reveal things that he otherwise would not to a dear disciple who loves him deeply. In other words, the mutual affection that exists between the disciple and the spiritual master instills in the guru a sense of obligation to pass on all the knowledge he possesses, even that which is most confidential.

One first begins on the path of devotion when one hears the powerful subjects related to Krishna from the mouth of a pure devotee.

The word *viśrambha* ("confidence, trust"), used by Srila Prabhupada as a synonym for *snigdha*, is also found elsewhere in the *Bhakti-rasāmṛta-sindhu* in the context of the guru-disciple relationship, where serving the spritual master with faith and trust is listed as one of the first elements of spiritual practice—*viśrambheṇa guroḥ sevā* (BRS 1.2.74).

The last point, finally, is that we should seek the association of devotees who are *svato vare*—more qualified than we ourselves in terms of scriptural knowledge, spiritual practice and character.

Relishing *the* Bhagavatam *with the* Rasika Devotees

When one has found such a person, who has tasted and thus knows the secrets of the life of devotion to Krishna, one relishes the Srimad Bhagavatam and seeks to understand its inner purport in his company. Srila Prabhupada comments on this, the second of these five most powerful devotional activities:

> We should seek the association of devotees who are more qualified than we ourselves in terms of scriptural knowledge, spiritual practice and character.

"One should then relish or seek out an essential understanding of the topics of the Bhagavatam in the company of rasika devotees. A rasika is a person who is experienced in the devotional life. This implies that one should not try to understand the Bhagavatam in other kinds of company, especially from Brahmins who follow various aspects of Vedic ritual but have abandoned the path of devotion, those who have a superficial understanding based on a purely academic knowledge of grammar and lexicography, those who keep the company of women and are completely absorbed in household life, those who are opposed to Vishnu and the Vaishnavas, the Mayavadis, offenders to the Holy Name, those who make their living by dressing up as Vaishnavas, reciting the Bhagavatam or giving initiation, or those who are only interested in their own sense gratification. Such people are incapable of understanding the purport of a scripture intended exclusively for the paramahamsas, so one should avoid studying the Bhagavata in their company, for the Sruti says that truths are revealed only to one who has as much faith in the guru as he has in God Himself, and the Smriti similarly says that the Bhagavatam can only be understood through devotion and never through one's own intelligence or by a lengthy study of many commentaries."

CC 2.22.127, Anubhāṣya

One should only study the Bhagavatam in the company of rasika devotees and not from those who are engaged in other kinds of religious practice, such as the Vedic ritualists. Even though they may be scholars and very learned in the linguistic aspects of the text, they will not be able to penetrate the essential message of devotion. Similarly the Mayavadis are inimical to the Lord and His devotees because they do not accept the eternal nature of devotion and its enactment in the Lord's lila. Srila Prabhupada here lists so many other devotional outsiders who may pose as saintly sadhus, but in whose company one cannot hope to enter into an understanding of devotional scriptures like the Bhagavatam. The *Śvetāśvatara Upaniṣad* states that the meaning of divine revelation comes only to those who have equal faith in the Lord and His manifestation in the world, the preceptor. One should therefore try to learn from such a faithful person.

yasya deve parā bhaktir
yathā deve tathā gurau
tasyaite kathitā hy arthāḥ
prakāśante mahātmanaḥ

> Only unto those great souls who have implicit faith in both the Lord and the spiritual master, who is His manifestation and not different from Him, are all the imports (*artha*) of Vedic knowledge automatically revealed. *Śvet U 6.23*

If we understand the word *artha* in the above verse to mean the *puruṣārtha* or "goal of human life," it becomes clearer, because only such a person who has faith in both the divine preceptor and the Supreme Lord will be able to understand the fifth and supreme goal of human life, which is love for the Lord.

Similarly, a famous verse of the Smriti states that the Bhagavatam can only be understood through devotion and never through one's own empirical intelligence or through reading many commentaries – *bhaktyā bhāgavataṁ grāhyaṁ na buddhyā na ca ṭīkayā*. All these warnings from the scripture indicate clearly that all these other pretenders have no qualification to enter into an understanding of the Bhagavatam, which is meant for the paramahamsa Vaishnavas alone. Those who are devotees in name only and who think that all these warnings are not meant for them cannot possibly enter into the Bhagavatam's meaning, because they have not understood the first thing about devotion and are therefore unqualified to relish this great text, which is the essence of all the Vedas and Vedanta.

If anyone should ask what need there is of understanding the finer details of theology (siddhanta), we need only look to the Chaitanya Charitamrita where Kaviraj Goswami says—

siddhānta baliye citte nā kara alasa
ihā haite kṛṣṇa lāge sudṛḍha mānasa

> Do not be lazy and neglect trying to understand the conclusions of the scriptures. The mind will become fixed on Krishna through a proper knowledge of siddhanta. *CC 1.2.117*

rasābhāsa haya jadi siddhānta-virodha
sahite nā pāre prabhu mane haya krodha

> If any statement contained perverted reflections of the transcendental aesthetic or went against the doctrines of the Bhagavatam, Mahaprabhu would find it intolerable and become angry. *CC 3.5.97*

Sri Chaitanya Mahaprabhu would feel very distressed if He heard anything that went against the scriptures or distorted the sentiments in Krishna's lila. For this reason, Swarup Damodar was charged with examining any material that was presented to Him. When instructing the Brahmin from East Bengal on how to perfect his spiritual life, Swarup Damodar said—

jāha bhāgavata paṛa vaiṣṇavera sthāne
ekānta āśraya kara caitanya-caraṇe
caitanya bhakta-gaṇera nitya kara saṅga
tabe ta jānibe siddhānta-samudra-taraṅga
tabe pāṇḍitya tomāra haibe saphala
kṛṣṇera svarūpa-līlā varṇibā nirmala

> Go and study the Bhagavatam from a Vaishnava. Take exclusive shelter of Chaitanya Mahaprabhu's lotus feet. Always seek the companionship of His devotees. If you do all this, you will be able to plunge into the ocean of His divine teachings. This will bring your scholarship to fruition. Then and then alone will you be able to describe Krishna's nature and pastimes purely. *CC 3.5.131-3*

Serving *the* Deity

The third of the five special devotional practices named in the *Bhakti-rasāmṛta-sindhu* is—

śraddhā-viśeṣataḥ prītiḥ
śrī-mūrter aṅghri-sevane

Srila Prabhupada comments on the special nature of deity worship (*śrī-mūrti-sevā*) as follows:

> As far as service to the Lord's deity form is concerned, the words *viśeṣataḥ prītiḥ* mean that one should not simply engage in the external formalities of deity worship, but should develop an enthusiasm for mentally serving the Divine Couple at every moment of the day or night. *CC 2.22.127, Anubhāṣya*

The immediate understanding of this particular devotional practice is given as "a love for serving the Lord in His deity form, arising out of a special kind of faith." Srila Prabhupada explains the words *śraddhā-viśeṣataḥ*, "a special kind of faith," in the following way: The ordinary, general kind of faith is engagement in the external activities of deity worship. Special faith refers to the mental service of the Divine Couple of the cowherd pastures. This same special kind of faith also applies to the way one engages in the other four activities.

If one has no faith in or love for serving the devotees, then one's service to the deity also becomes mundane.

Devotee association is also absolutely imperative for anyone wishing to perfect service to the Lord's deity form. If one has no faith in or love for serving the devotees, then one's service to the deity also becomes mundane; such a worshiper remains on the lowest rungs of devotional service. One who has faith in the devotees rises to the middle level of devotional life. When one sees the devotee on the highest platform, one automatically becomes joyous and the Holy Name spontaneously appears on his lips. No doubt such highly elevated devotees are very rare. Whatever the case, the Lord is more satisfied when His devotee is served than when He Himself receives service. He says *mad-bhakta-pūjābhyadhikā*. If someone worships Krishna but does not worship the devotee, Krishna does not accept it, but calls this low-level devotee a hypocrite. Lord Nrisingha Deva says that on His feast day, Nrisingha Chaturdasi, we must offer worship to His devotee Prahlada before doing anything else. We also saw earlier that offering the Lord's remnants to His eternal associates like Vishwaksen and the other Vaishnavas is an integral part of puja.

This is why the Chaitanya Charitamrita places so much emphasis on the dust of the devotees' feet, the water that has washed their feet, and the remnants of their foodstuffs, calling them "the strength of our spiritual practice" and "the givers of love for Krishna." The Lord subordinates Himself to the love of His devotees and therefore gives the worship of His devotees the highest place in the domain of devotional practice.

CHANTING *the* HOLY NAME

Regarding chanting of the Holy Name, here Srila Prabhupada only says, "One should chant the Holy Name, i.e., one should chant a fixed number of rounds every day, controlling the mind by concentrating on the sound vibration." Chaitanya Mahaprabhu's dear associate Jagadananda Pandit stresses the part association plays in chanting the Holy Name:

asādhu-saṅgete bhāi nāma nāhi haya
nāmākṣara bāhirāya baṭe nāma kabhu naya
kabhu nāmābhāsa sadā haya nāma aparādha
e saba jānibe bhāi kṛṣṇa-bhaktir bādha
jadi karibe kṛṣṇa-nāma sādhu-saṅga kara
bhukti-mukti-siddhi-vāñchā dūre parihara

O brother! You cannot chant the Holy Name in the association of non-devotees. The sound of the Holy Name may come out of your mouth, but it will not really be the Name. It will sometimes be the Name's reflection (*nāmābhāsa*) and sometimes offensive chanting (*nāmāparādha*), but you should know, O brother, that in either case, this kind of chanting interferes with the attainment of pure devotion to Krishna. If you want to chant the Holy Names, then associate with devotees and keep desires for sense enjoyment, liberation and yogic powers at a distance.
Prema-vivarta 7.1-3

This statement shows that if one wants to engage in devotional life, chanting the Holy Name or hearing the Srimad Bhagavatam, he should find devotees who are free from desires for material sense enjoyment or liberation, who do everything they can to avoid situations that are inimical to devotion and to seek situations that are favorable. Jagadananda Pandit thus goes on to say,

sādhu saṅga kṛṣṇa nāme ei mātra cāi
saṁsāra jinite āra kono vastu nāi
bhajite bhajite kṛṣṇa pāda-padma pāi

All I want in life is to chant Hare Krishna in the company of devotees, for nothing is equal to this for overcoming the material entanglement. By chanting continuously, I will attain Krishna's lotus feet. *PV 6.13, 11*

The conclusion, then, is that if we want to chant the Holy Name purely, without offenses, it is essential to keep the company of advanced Vaishnavas.

RESIDING *in the* HOLY DHAMA

Srila Prabhupada makes the following comment on residing in Mathura, the fifth and last of the most powerful devotional activities:

One should reside in Mathura, the land where Krishna lived. By extension, the land of Gauda where Chaitanya Mahaprabhu appeared is also a divine land, and thus one may equally take up residence in Sri Mayapur Dham. Jagannath Puri and other places in South India visited by Mahaprabhu are also to be considered non-different from Vrindavan. Even if you should live in Vrindavan, if you consider these other holy places to be different from Vrindavan or Mathura, you are in material consciousness and will fall down. *CC 2.22.127, Anubhāṣya*

Thus the injunction to reside in Mathura extends to residence in the other holy places connected to Krishna's activities in His incarnation as Lord Chaitanya. As Narottam Das sings in *Prema-bhakti-candrikā*—

śrī gauḍa maṇḍala bhūmi jebā jāne cintāmaṇi
tāra haya vraja-bhūme vāsa

He verily lives in Vrindavan who knows that Gauda, the land along the banks of the Bhagirathi River, is transcendental.

Jagannath Puri and other places in South India are considered sacred because they were visited by Lord Sri Chaitanya Mahaprabhu. One who makes distinctions between these various places, even if he should take up residence in

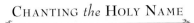

Mathura, will not attain the full benefit of life in the Dham because his vision of it is mundane. Bhaktivinode Thakur has also glorified the holiness of Nabadwip Dham in song:

gauḍa-vraja-vane bheda nā dekhibo
haiba baraja-vāsī
dhāmera svarūpa sphuribe nayane
haiba rādhāra dāsī

When I no longer see any distinction between the lands of Gauda and Vraja, then I will become an eternal resident of Vraja Dham. The true form of the Lord's holy abode will be revealed before my eyes and I will become Radharani's dasi.

Gīta-mālā, Siddhi-lālasā, 1

Whether one lives in the region of Mathura or Gauda Mandala, one must reside there in the community of devotees. Bhaktivinode Thakur says:

gaura āmāra je saba sthāna
karala bhramaṇa raṅge
se saba sthāna heraba āmi
praṇayi bhakata-saṅge

I shall joyfully visit all the places where my beloved Gauranga wandered, relishing the company of His ecstatic loving devotees. *Śaraṇāgati*

As we have already seen, the benefit of visiting any holy place is derived principally from meeting the holy persons who live there.

bhavad-vidhā bhāgavatās
tīrtha-bhūtāḥ svayaṁ vibho
tīrthī-kurvanti tīrthāni
svāntaḥ-sthena gadābhṛtā

Great devotees like yourself are yourselves places of pilgrimage. Indeed, you make the places of pilgrimage truly holy, for you carry the Lord in your heart.

SB 1.13.10

Bhaktivinode Thakur writes in *Kalyāṇa-kalpa-taru*—

tīrtha phala sādhu-saṅga
sādhu saṅge antaraṅga
śrī-kṛṣṇa-bhajana manohara
yathā sādhu tathā tīrtha
sthira kari nija-citta
sādhu-saṅga kara ataḥ para

The benefit of visiting holy places is the association of saintly devotees. When one has the association of devotees, then one can engage in the pleasing service of the Lord more intimately. Bear always in mind that the true holy places are wherever saintly persons live. Knowing this, you should give precedence to keeping saintly company.

ye tīrthete vaiṣṇava nāi se tīrthete nāhi yāi
ki lābha hāṅṭiyā dūra deśa
yathāya vaiṣṇava gaṇa sei sthāna vṛndāvana
sei sthāne ānanda aśeṣa

I never visit a place of pilgrimage where there is no Vaishnava. Otherwise, what profit is there in travelling to far-off lands? Wherever Vaishnavas assemble, that is Vrindavan and that is where I shall find unlimited joy. *KKT 14*

Lord Chaitanya revealed the same truth in His pastime of visiting the famous pilgrimage site Gaya, where He encountered His spritual master, Ishwar Puri. As soon as the two of them saw each other, they both were overwhelmed by waves of ecstatic love for Krishna. Mahaprabhu then told Ishwar Puri that His actual purpose in coming to Gaya had been to meet him—

prabhu bale—gayā yātrā saphala āmāra
yata kṣaṇe dekhilāṅ caraṇa tomāra
tīrthe piṇḍa dile se nistare pitṛ gaṇa
seha yāre piṇḍa deya tare sei jana
tomā dekhile-i mātra koṭi pitṛ gaṇa
sei kṣaṇe sarva bandha pāya vimocana
ataeva tīrtha nahe tomāra samāna
tīrthero parama tumi maṅgala pradhāna
saṁsāra samudra haite uddhāraha more
ei āmi deha samarpilāṅ tomāre
kṛṣṇa-pāda-padmera amṛta rasa pāna
āmāre karāo tumi ei cāhi dāna

> "My trip to Gaya became a success as soon as I saw your lotus feet. One who comes here to offer oblations delivers his forefathers and perhaps himself as well. As soon as I saw you, however, millions of forefathers were immediately delivered from their material bondage. No holy place could ever be your equal. Indeed, saints like you are the only real reason any holy place has the power to sanctify sinners. Please lift Me out of this ocean of material entanglement. I hereby surrender My body and life to you. All I ask of you is that you please give Me the nectar of Krishna's lotus feet to drink." *Cbh 1.17.50-55*

Chaitanya Mahaprabhu is the world teacher and we can all profit from this instruction. The greatest benefit that comes of visiting places of pilgrimage is to meet the holy persons who frequent them. We will only feel the need to engage in pious activities such as visiting holy places or giving in charity, mundane rituals like offering oblations to the deceased, or various types of meditative practices, until we have surrendered to a bona fide spiritual master and tasted the sweetness of service to the Supreme Lord. One who makes offerings to the forefathers at Gaya will only liberate the beneficiary of the ritual, but on simply seeing the spiritual master, a Vaishnava, or other holy person, millions and millions of forefathers are liberated. Therefore, no one should think that visiting a place of pilgrimage is ever equal to coming into contact with a pure devotee, spiritual master or a Vaishnava. The spiritual master is so powerful that he can bestow on us a taste for the nectar of Krishna's lotus feet, the highest purpose in life.

Visiting a place of pilgrimage is never equal to coming into contact with a pure devotee spiritual master or a Vaishnava.

Chapter 6

Desirable *and* Undesirable Association

Sri Chaitanya Mahaprabhu's teaching is that the one and only thing we should pray for is pure devotional service to the Divine Couple of Vrindavan, Sri Sri Radha Madhava. Therefore, the Gaudiya Vaishnavas remember and take very seriously statements like *bhaktis tu bhagavad-bhakta-saṅgena parijāyate*, "Devotion to the Lord arises out of association with His devotees," and *kṛṣṇa-bhakti-janma-mūla haya sādhu-saṅga*, "The root cause of devotion is the association of devotees." In accordance with authoritative statements such as these, the Gaudiya Vaishnava acharyas tell us that it is an absolute necessity for a person who has taken initiation from a bona fide spiritual master and is eager to advance in spiritual life and attain pure bhajan to associate with saintly persons who are more advanced than himself and who share the same desire, the same object of devotion. These devotees should be affectionate; they should possess deep attachment to the disciplic succession and its goals; they should take delight in the practice of bhajan; and they should know the esoteric secrets connected to devotional life and be able to impart them.

We should only keep company with those whose qualities we aspire to develop.

We are all influenced by the company we keep. In the *Hari-bhakti-sudhodaya*, Hiranyakashipu tells Prahlada—

yasya yat-saṅgatiḥ puṁso
maṇivat syāt sa tad-guṇaḥ
sva-kula-rddhyai tato dhīmān
sva-yūthān eva saṁśrayet

Like a glass crystal, a person takes on the qualities of those with whom he comes in contact. One who is intelligent should therefore seek the company of those who have the same ideals in order to develop their good qualities in himself.

BRS 1.2.229

When one places a red hibiscus in front of a crystal, the crystal turns red. The same thing happens to us when we keep the company of others—their qualities and their flaws are transmitted to us. For this reason, we should only keep company with those whose qualities we aspire to develop. The words *sva-yūthān* here are synonymous with *sajātīya*, "having the same aspirations."

There are many who, when it comes to taking initiation, hearing the chanting of the Holy Name, listening to the recital of the Srimad Bhagavatam, and visiting or living in the Holy Dham, are lax in their inquiries and in the association they keep. But the result of such carelessness is that they very quickly fall from the path of devotional service.

VAISHNAVA BEHAVIOR MEANS AVOIDING UNHOLY COMPANY

When giving lessons to Sanatan Goswami, Mahaprabhu summarized the essence of Vaishnava behavior in the following couplet—

asat-saṅga-tyāga ei vaiṣṇava ācāra
strī-saṅgī eka asādhu kṛṣṇābhakta āra

> The rejection of unholy company is the essence of Vaishnava behavior. The unholy are divided into those addicted to sex life and those who oppose the principle of devotion to Krishna. *CC 2.22.87*

Srila Bhaktivinode Thakur writes in the *Amṛta-pravāha-bhāṣya*, "Just as the positive injunction of Vaishnava behavior is to associate with saintly devotees, the negative injunction or prohibition is to avoid bad company."

Srila Prabhupada further explains this in his *Anubhāṣya* to this verse:

"The principal, indeed, vital element in Vaishnava behavior is to reject bad association. The 'bad' are here described as belonging to two categories: those who keep the company of women and those who are not devotees. The 'company of women' is of two kinds: One is morally acceptable, as it is within the Varnashram socio-religious system; indeed, it is the very foundation of Varnashram. The second is immoral and against the principles of religion; it undermines the Varnashram social system and thus has terrible consequences for anyone who engages in it. Someone who is engaged in sinful activities in this world is completely undeserving of the name Vaishnava. Non-Vaishnava or immoral behavior is intertwined with the three goals of life known as dharma, artha and kama. Even though the fourth goal of liberation does not derive from the association of women, it still leads one away from Krishna and thus one who desires it is an even greater non-Vaishnava and a more dangerous companion than the person obsessed by sex. One who denies the reality of the world is a Mayavadi, whereas one who embraces the world as a source of enjoyment is called a *māyā-vilāsī*.

"The company of either one of these kinds of asadhu is destructive to one's own development of Vaishnava qualities and character, or pure devotion. The Mayavadi desires liberation, to which end he gives up material sense gratification, but this is also a selfish objective as he seeks only to set himself apart as something superior. The person who finds pleasure in the company of women is a seeker of sense enjoyment; he is described as a *bhogi*, or sensualist. Both of these kinds of people are ultimately seeking something separate from Krishna—their personal pleasure. Being full of deception and hypocrisy, they are never worthy of the title 'servant of Krishna.'"

CC 2.22.87, Amrita-pravāha-bhāsya

It is thus not advisable to seek out the company of those who, even though pious, are still beset with desires for sense enjoyment, liberation or spiritual powers. In answer to the Lord's questions, Ramananda Raya said—

mukti bhukti vāñche jei
kāṅhā duṅhāra gati
sthāvara-deha deva-deha
jaiche avasthiti

> "What end do those who desire liberation meet? And what is the destination of those who seek sense gratification?
>
> "The first take birth as an immobile entity like a tree, while the latter take birth amongst the demigods." *CC 2.8.256*

In his *Anubhāṣya* to this verse, Srila Prabhupada writes, "In their search for liberation, the Mayavadis give up material sense gratification, but ultimately they also give up the possibility of pure spiritual action. They take birth as entities whose consciousness is dormant, such as trees or other non-moving beings. The highest achievement of the sensualists, who take material sense gratification to be the ultimate purpose of life, is to attain a demigod body."

Therefore, Narottam Das, the best of the acharyas to follow in the footsteps of Sri Rupa Goswami and Swarup Damodar Goswami, loudly proclaims in his *Prema-bhakti-candrikā*—

karmī jñānī miche bhakta
nā habe tāya anurakta
śuddha-bhajanete kara mon
vraja-janera jei mata
tāhe hobo anugata
ei sei parama-tattva dhana

Do not get attached to the company of materialists, dry philosophers or false devotees, but apply yourself to pure bhajan. I will always follow the opinions of the Vraja devotees, for that is the highest wealth of devotional truth.

karma-kāṇḍa jñāna-kāṇḍa
kevala viṣera bhāṇḍa
amṛta boliyā jebā khāya
nānā yoni bhrame mare
kadarya bhakṣaṇa kare
tāra janma adhaḥpāte jāya

The paths of ritualism and philosophical speculation are nothing but reservoirs of poison. Those who drink of them, thinking that they are the nectar of immortality, end up taking birth again and again, wandering through the creation, eating the inedible, and sinking ever lower and lower.

The Definition *of* Pure Devotional Service

The essence of the Srimad Bhagavatam is summarized by Rupa Goswami in his definition of the highest state of devotion, in which he specifically mentions that jnana and karma obscure pure bhakti—

anyābhilāṣitā-śūnyaṁ
jñāna-karmādy-anāvṛtam
ānukūlyena kṛṣṇānu-
śīlanaṁ bhaktir uttamā

The highest category of devotion or bhakti is the culture of a favorable attitude to Krishna, devoid of all material desires and without any adulteration by monistic philosophy or fruitive action, or any other activity that opposes pure devotion. *BRS 1.1.11; CC 2.19.167*

Srila Prabhupada has explained this verse in his *Anubhāṣya* (2.19.167), where he gives a word-by-word Sanskrit language commentary of the verse:

"*Anyābhilāṣitā-śūnyam* means 'completely free of all desires for immoral activities like sexual promiscuity, which lead one away from perfecting the worship of Krishna.' *Jñāna-karmādy-anāvṛtam*. *Jñāna* here means the philosophical search that leads to oneness with the impersonal aspect of the Lord and not the use of reason to seek out the personal object of worship. *Karma* refers to the ritual activities and other regular and occasional religious duties enjoined in the Smritis, and not to the activities of devotional service like worshiping the Lord's deity form. Both of these are aspects of the cultivation of a favorable attitude to Krishna. The word *ādi* refers to other spiritual activities that are similarly unhelpful to the attainment of a consciousness of Krishna. *Anāvṛtam* means uncovered, i.e., not interrupted by any of these. *Ānukūlyena* ('favorably') means activity that is intended to please Krishna. *Prātikūlyena* would be its opposite, meaning activities which, even though directed at Krishna, are not intended for His pleasure, or anything else that impedes the attainment of devotion. The word *kṛṣṇānuśīlanam* means the constant engagement of the body, mind and words in activities for the pleasure of Krishna, the Supreme Personality of Godhead, or His expansions in multifarious Vishnu tattva forms. *Sā uttamā bhaktiḥ*—this is the definition of the highest devotional service, which applies whether such devotion is impelled by scriptural injunction and logical arguments, as in *vaidhī bhakti*, or by spontaneous desire, as in *rāgānugā bhakti*, whether

on the stage of practice or on the stage of achievement of the goal."

This topmost devotion leads to love for Krishna. Rupa Goswami therefore begins his discourse on devotion with this definition. Srila Krishna Das Kaviraj explains the verse in Bengali with the following couplets—

anya vāñchā anya pūjā chāḍi jñāna karma
ānukūlye sarvendriye kṛṣṇānuśīlana
ei śuddha bhakti ihā haite prema haya
pañcarātre bhāgavate ei lakṣaṇa kaya

Both the Pancharatra and the Bhagavata describe pure devotional service as the engagement of all the senses in the favorable cultivation of Krishna consciousness, abandoning all other desires and all other worshipable objects; abandoning ritualistic religious practices or philosophical speculation. Through such pure devotion, one attains prema.
CC 2.19.168-169

Bhaktivinode Thakur has commented on this passage in his *Amṛta-pravāha-bhāṣya:* "The sign of pure devotion is that when one has taken to the path, one can have no desire for anything other than advancing further along it. It is not possible for one to engage in the worship of any aspect of the Lord such as Brahman or Paramatma when one is dedicated exclusively to Krishna, nor to engage in activities like the culture of philosophical knowledge or works that have sense pleasure and liberation as their goal, even though the cultivation of knowledge of sambandha, abhidheya and prayojana and works that lead to the pleasure of the Lord are desirable. When one is freed from all these undesirable distractions and leads his life in such a way that it is conducive for devotion, engaging all the senses in the culture of Krishna is known as pure devotion."

These characteristics of pure devotion to the Lord are accepted in both the Bhagavatam and the Pancharatra literature. Srila Rupa Goswami points out the oneness of these two Vaishnava traditions by quoting the Pancharatra definition of bhakti—

sarvopādhi-vinirmuktaṁ
tat-paratvena nirmalam
hṛṣīkeṇa hṛṣīkeśa-
sevanaṁ bhaktir ucyate

Bhakti is defined as the engagement of the senses in the service of the Proprietor of the Senses. This service is to be free from any contamination by identity with the body, and pure through being exclusively fixed on Him. *BRS 1.1.12*

Here, the essential characteristic of devotion is the engagement of all the senses in the service of the Master of the Senses. Two contingent characteristics of devotion are named in support of this essential one: that it is free from any false identity and, being fixed on Krishna, is entirely pure.

The Bhagavatam also gives the following definition of pure devotion—

mad-guṇa-śruti-mātreṇa
mayi sarva-guhāśaye
mano-gatir avicchinnā
yathā gaṅgāmbhaso'mbudhau

lakṣaṇaṁ bhakti-yogasya
nirguṇasya hy udāhṛtam
ahaituky avyavahitā
yā bhaktiḥ puruṣottame

The primary sign that pure union in devotion, free from any material quality, has appeared in someone's heart comes when, upon hearing about My qualities, the devotee's thoughts are drawn immediately and irresistably towards Me, the indweller of all beings, in the same way that the waters of the Ganges flow toward the sea. Like the flow of the Ganges, such devotion to the Supreme Person is both unmotivated and unimpeded. *SB 3.29.10-11*

Ahaitukī ("unmotivated") means that the devotion is spontaneous and natural, while *avyavahitā* ("unimpeded") means that it is uninterrupted or undisturbed by ulterior motives.

sālokya-sārṣṭi-sāmīpya-
sārūpyaikatvam apy uta
dīyamānaṁ na gṛhṇanti
vinā mat-sevanaṁ janāḥ

sa eva bhakti-yogākhya
ātyantika udāhṛtaḥ
yenātivrajya tri-guṇaṁ
mad-bhāvāyopapadyate

Unless he is assured of having service to the Lord, a pure devotee does not accept any kind of liberation, whether it be residence on the same planet as the Lord, having opulences equal to His, being in proximity to Him, having a form like His, or monistic union—even though the Lord may offer all these things to him.

Thus have I described the superlative stage of that which is known as bhakti yoga. By mastering this discipline, one can overcome the three qualities of material nature and attain true feeling (*bhāva*) for Me. *SB 3.29.12-13*

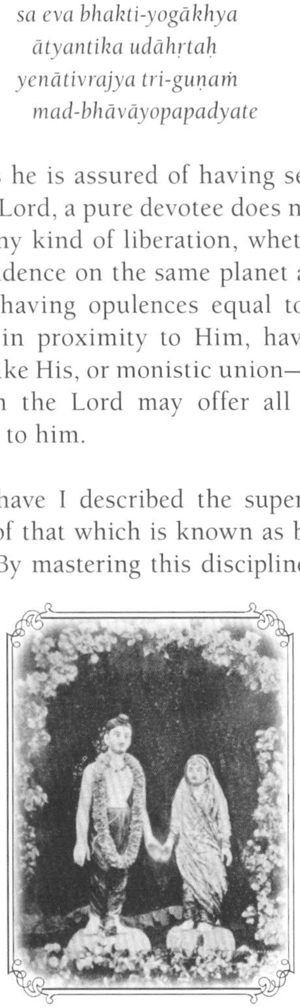

Bhaktivinode Thakur points out in his *Amṛta-pravāha-bhāṣya* that the devotion described here has been called *ātyantika* ("superlative, ultimate"), meaning that it takes the practitioner beyond the material modes of nature and bestows pure, ecstatic love of Krishna on him or her.

In view of all this, when we make decisions about the kind of company we want to keep, we should avoid those who merely pose as sadhus while harboring desires for sense gratification or liberation. If we truly desire devotion to Krishna above all, then how can we say that such people have the same aspirations (*sajātīyāśaya*) as we? If we are engaged in genuine sadhu sanga, such superficial desires will never be able to touch our essential being.

The MAYAVADI *is* UNDESIRABLE ASSOCIATION

A devotee thinks that nothing is more inimical to the attainment of pure devotion than total union with the impersonal aspect of God.

sāyujya śunite bhakter ghṛṇā lajjā bhaya
naraka vāñchaye tabu sāyujya nā laya
brahme īśvare sāyujya dui ta prakāra
brahma sāyujya haite īśvara sāyujya dhikkāra

The devotee feels disgust, shame and fear when he hears talk of merging into Narayan. He will go to hell before accepting the liberation of sayujya. There are two kinds of sayujya mukti. One can merge either into the impersonal Brahman or into the Supreme Lord. The latter is even more reprehensible than the former. *CC 2.6.268-9*

Bhaktivinode Thakur comments on these verses in his *Amṛta-pravāha-bhāṣya:* "Sayujya is of two kinds—either merging into the form of the personal God or into His impersonal aspect. The former is the goal of yogis like Patanjali and is called *kaivalya*. The Mayavadi followers of the Vedanta consider merging into the impersonal aspect of the Lord to be the ultimate goal of life. Of the two, the desire to merge directly into the form of the personal God is even more detestable to the devotees than desiring to merge into His impersonal aspect. One who meditates on the impersonal Brahman becomes one with the undifferentiated, all-pervading spiritual substratum of creation, Brahman. The yogi, however, meditates on the personal form of God with the hope of becoming absorbed into His existence. This is the result of a corruption of desire and leads to even greater downfall."

When Mahaprabhu was living in Jagannath Puri, He had a renounced and humble associate named Bhagavan Acharya. Once, Bhagavan Acharya's younger brother Gopal Bhattacharya came to visit him in Puri after studying Shankara's commentary to the Vedanta in Benares. When Bhagavan Acharya took his brother to see Mahaprabhu, the Lord, being the indweller of all souls, recognized that Gopal was not a true Vaishnava and so did not feel any great pleasure in his company. Nevertheless, because of His love for Bhagavan Acharya, the Lord was polite and friendly to his brother.

The devotee feels disgust, shame and fear when he hears talk of merging into Narayan. He will go to hell before accepting the liberation of sayujya.

Despite the Lord's coolness toward Gopal, Bhagavan Acharya approached Swarup Damodar and said, "My brother has studied Vedanta in Benares and would like to give a lecture on it. Would you and the other devotees be kind enough to attend?" Swarup Damodar was the acharya's friend and so he spoke to him frankly. With anger tempered by love, he said—

buddhi-bhraṣṭa haila tomāra gopālera saṅge
māyāvāda śunibāre upajila raṅge
vaiṣṇava hañā jebā śārīraka-bhāṣya śune
sevya-sevaka-bhāva chāḍi āpanāre īśvara māne
mahā-bhāgavata jei kṛṣṇa prāṇa-dhana jāra
māyāvāda-śravaṇe citta avaśya phire tāṅra

"Your brother's company has made you lose your intelligence, and so you now think it would be fun to listen to Mayavada philosophy. When a Vaishnava listens to Shankara's commentary on *Vedānta-sūtra*, the *Śārīraka-bhāṣya*, he stops making a distinction between master and servant and starts thinking that he himself is the Supreme Lord. Hearing the Mayavada philosophy will unfailingly change the mentality of even a Maha Bhagavata devotee, whose life and soul is Krishna." *CC 3.2.94-96*

Even though he had been admonished by him, Bhagavan Acharya continued to try to convince Swarup Damodar. He said, "Mahaprabhu's devotees are all completely attached to Krishna's lotus feet. How could listening to the *Śārīraka-bhāṣya* possibly dislodge them from their one and only refuge?"

Swarup Damodar answered with a further warning about the adverse effects of the impersonalist teachings. He said, "When we hear the Mayavada philosophy, we not only gain no positive spiritual understanding, but we are told that Brahman is the only spiritual reality and the universe created by Him is entirely false. It breaks a devotee's heart to hear a Mayavadi say that the living entity's separate existence is only imaginary and that the personal God is also a manifestation of ignorance." *CC 3.2.98-99*

Thakur Bhaktivinode has commented on this story in the *Amṛta-pravāha-bhāṣya*: "Shankaracharya's commentary on the Vedanta Sutra is known as the *Śarīraka-bhāṣya*. If he hears this *Śarīraka-bhāṣya*, which is full of the impersonalist philosophy, the devotional attitude of even a Maha Bhagavata, one who treasures Lord Krishna on the deepest levels of realization, will inevitably deteriorate and he will fall from the devotional standard. Swarup Damodar thus said that even though a devotee may think that since he is fully committed to Krishna and that hearing Shankara's commentaries cannot shake his faith, it is still natural for him to feel pain on hearing its doctrines—i.e., that the Supreme Truth is formless and that the form of Krishna is an imaginary creation produced of the illusory energy. So what could possibly induce a devotee to listen to it?"

Bhagavan Acharya finally understood what Swarup Damodar was getting at and felt shame for having asked the devotees to listen to a philosophy that went so deeply against their principles. Not long afterward he asked his brother to return home.

The UNDESIRABLE ASSOCIATION *of the* SEXUALLY PROMISCUOUS

The other kind of bad association is described by Lord Kapila Deva in his instructions to his mother Devahuti, where he tells of the terrible consequences of excessive attachment to sexuality:

satyaṁ śaucaṁ dayā maunaṁ
buddhir hrīḥ śrīr yaśaḥ kṣamā
śamo damo bhagaś ceti
yat-saṅgād yāti saṅkṣayam

teṣv aśānteṣu mūḍheṣu
khaṇḍitātmasv asādhuṣu
saṅgaṁ na kuryāc chocyeṣu
yoṣit-krīḍā-mṛgeṣu ca

na tathāsya bhaven moho
bandhaś cānya-prasaṅgataḥ
yoṣit-saṅgād yathā puṁso
yathā tat-saṅgi-saṅgataḥ

One should avoid association at all costs with those lamentable creatures who have become the playthings of women. They are lacking in peace, are constantly bewildered, and their concept of self is fragmented. Indeed there is no enchantment more powerful, no bondage surer for a man than that which comes through the association of women or of those addicted to women. By keeping such company, one loses twelve qualities: truthfulness, internal and external cleanliness, mercy, gravity, intelligence, modesty, beauty both physical and spiritual, good reputation, forgiveness, control of the mind and senses, and good fortune. *SB 3.31.33-35*

Nevertheless, it is clear that the past acharyas always considered the association of the Mayavadi to be far worse than that of the mere sensualist. Bhaktivinode Thakur sings:

viṣaya-vimūḍha āra māyāvādī jana
bhakti-śūnya duṅhe prāṇa dhare akāraṇa

Both those who are bewildered by the promise of sense enjoyments and Mayavadi impersonalists are devoid of devotion. Their lives have no purpose.

ei dui saṅga nātha nā haya āmāra
prārthanā kariye āmi caraṇe tomāra

I pray at your feet, O Lord, that I never be subjected to the association of either one or the other.

se duera madhye viṣayī tabe bhāla
māyāvādī-saṅga nāhi māgi kona kāla

Of the two, however, I would rather be with a sensualist than with a Mayavadi, to whose company I hope I will never be subjected.

viṣayī-hṛdaya jabe sādhu-saṅga pāya
anāyāse labhe bhakti bhaktera kṛpāya

A sensualist may be transformed by the association of a devotee, whose mercy can easily turn him to a life of devotion.

māyāvāda doṣa jāra hṛdaya paśila
kutarke hṛdaya tāra vajra-sama bhela

On the other hand, once the heart has been touched by the impersonalist contamination, it becomes covered by a carapace of false arguments and turns as hard as stone.

वासुदेव घोष
नवद्वीप योगपीठ

bhaktira svarūpa āra viṣaya āśraya
māyāvādī anitya boliyā saba kaya

The Mayavadi considers devotion itself, the devotee, and the object of devotion all to be temporary manifestations of the material world.

dhik tāra kṛṣṇa-sevā śravaṇa-kīrtana
kṛṣṇa aṅge vajra hāne tāhāra stavana

I curse the Mayavadi's so-called service to Krishna, his hearing of the Bhagavatam and his chanting of the Holy Names. His prayers are like thunderbolts on Krishna's body.

māyāvāda sama bhakti pratikūla nāi
ataeva māyāvāda saṅga nāhi cāi

There is nothing more harmful to devotion than Mayavada. I do not, therefore, wish to ever keep company with anyone who subscribes to that philosophy.

bhakativinoda māyāvāda dūra kari
vaiṣṇava-saṅgete baise nāmāśraya dhari

Bhaktivinode hereby rejects the Mayavada doctrine and takes shelter of the Holy Names in the association of devotees. *Śaraṇāgati 27*

So, whatever one's external qualifications in terms of social status, education or renunciation, if he is opposed to the service of the Lord, his association should be scrupulously avoided. The *Kātyāyana-saṁhitā* warns:

varaṁ huta-vaha-jvālā-
pañjarāntar-vyavasthitiḥ
na śauri-cintā-vimukha-
jana-saṁvāsa-vaiśasam

Better to be locked in a cage surrounded by burning flames than to suffer in the association of those who dislike thinking of Krishna. *HBV 10.295; CC 2.22.88*

mā drākṣīḥ kṣīṇa-puṇyān kvacid api
bhagavad-bhakti-hīnān manuṣyān

Never look upon those persons who are bereft of devotion to the Lord and whose pious merit has thus dwindled to nothingness. *CC 2.22.89*

CASTE *is* NOT *a* CONSIDERATION *when* CHOOSING VAISHNAVA ASSOCIATION

Vrindavan Das Thakur says in the Chaitanya Bhagavata:

brāhmaṇa haiyā jadi avaiṣṇava haya
tabe tāra ālāpe-o puṇya jāya kṣaya

To even converse with a Brahmin who

is not a Vaishnava erodes all one's accumulated good deeds. *Cbh 1.16.305*

He supports his statement with quotes from the Padma Purana:

kim atra bahunoktena
brāhmaṇā ye'py avaiṣṇavāḥ
teṣāṁ sambhāṣaṇaṁ sparśaṁ
pramādenāpi varjayet
śvapākam iva nekṣeta
loke vipram avaiṣṇavam
vaiṣṇavo varṇa-bāhyo'pi
punāti bhuvana-trayam

What need is there for a long discourse on the subject? Even a Brahmin who is not a Vaishnava should be avoided: one should not talk to him; one should not touch him, even by mistake. Just as one should not even look at an untouchable, so too one should not even look at a Brahmin who is not a Vaishnava. On the other hand, a Vaishnava purifies the three worlds, no matter what caste he belongs to—even if he is an outcaste. *Cbh 1.16.303-304*

In these verses, anyone who is not engaged in devotional service to the Lord is classified as a non-Vaishnava. Even though the scripture says the Brahmin is spiritual master to all the other castes (*varṇānāṁ brāhmaṇo guru*)—a Brahmin who is devoid of devotion to Vishnu is not acceptable as a spiritual master. There are many other statements confirming this in the Vaishnava scriptures:

mahā-kūla-prasūto'pi
sarva-yajñeṣu dīkṣitaḥ
sahasra-śākhādhyāyī ca
na guruḥ syād avaiṣṇavaḥ

Though born in a noble family and initiated in the performance of all the sacrifices, even if he has studied every one of the thousands of branches of revealed scripture, a man is still not qualified to be guru if he is not a Vaishnava. *HBV 1.54*

In this case, though, the *Hari-bhakti-vilāsa*

gives the most basic definition of "Vaishnava":

gṛhīta-viṣṇu-dīkṣāko
viṣṇu-pūjā-paro naraḥ
vaiṣṇavo'bhihito'bhijñair
itaro'smād avaiṣṇavaḥ

A person who has taken initiation in the Vishnu mantra from a qualified guru and is engaged in serving the Lord in His deity form is called a Vaishnava by the wise. Anyone who does not fit this description is a non-Vaishnava. *HBV 1.55*

On the other hand, because association with devotees is so important, we must be careful not to allow their physical or superficial traits to distract us from their essential characteristic, which is devotion. The Lord gave no importance to any qualification other than devotion—not learning, family background, class, wealth or anything else. There are many verses that support this understanding.

nīca-jāti nahe kṛṣṇa-bhajanera ayogya
sat-kula-vipra nahe bhajanera yogya
je bhaje se baṛa abhakta hīna chāra
kṛṣṇa-bhajane nāhi jāti-kulādi vicāra

Someone born in a low caste is not disqualified from worshiping Krishna, while one born as a pious Brahmin is not especially qualified to worship Him. The one who worships Krishna is the superior person, whereas one who does not is inferior. There is no consideration of birth or background in the worship of the Lord. *CC 3.4.66-7*

je te kule vaiṣṇavera janma kene nahe
tathāpiha sarva-vandya sarva-śāstre kahe

A Vaishnava is worshipable to all, no matter what kind of family he has been born into. This is the verdict of all the scriptures. *Cbh 2.10.100*

jāti kula saba nirarthaka bujhāite
janmilena haridāsa adhama kulete

In order to prove to the world that caste or family background have no relevance to one's spiritual life, Hari Das took birth in a lowly family. *Cbh 1.16.237*

kibā vipra kibā nyāsī śūdra kene naya
yei kṛṣṇa tattva vettā sei guru haya

A person who knows the truths of spiritual life is qualified to be guru, whether he is a Brahmin, a sannyasi or a shudra. *CC 2.8.128*

caṇḍālo'pi dvija-śreṣṭho
hari-bhakti-parāyaṇaḥ
hari-bhakti-vihīnaś ca
dvijo'pi śvapacādhamaḥ

The lowest outcaste becomes equal to the best Brahmin if he is fixed in devotion to Lord Hari. On the other hand, a Brahmin who is devoid of devotion is worse than the lowest outcaste.

This is just a small selection of scriptural texts that demonstrate what is truly important in the eyes of the Lord concerning His devotee.

We should thus seek out the association of Vaishnavas who are not deceivers, who are more advanced than ourselves, who have similar objectives in spiritual life, who are affectionate, and who are expert in the life of devotion. Narottam Das shows us how to pray for such Vaishnava association:

ṭhākura vaiṣṇava-pada, avanīra su-sampada,
śuna bhāi hañā eka mana
āśraya laiyā bhaje, tāre kṛṣṇa nāhi tyaje,
āra saba mare akāraṇa

The lotus feet of the saintly Vaishnavas are this world's greatest treasure. O my dear brothers! Please listen attentively. Krishna never forsakes one who worships Him after taking refuge of the Vaishnavas. All others live and die uselessly.

vaiṣṇava-caraṇa-jala, prema bhakti dite bala,
āra keha nahe balavanta
vaiṣṇava-caraṇa-renu, mastake bhūṣaṇa binu,
āra nāhi bhuṣaṇera anta

The water that has washed the feet of a Vaishnava has the power to give divine love for Krishna. Nothing else is equal to it in strength. I need no decoration other than the dust of the feet of the Vaishnavas.

tīrtha-jala pavitra-guṇa, likhiyāche purāṇe,
se saba bhaktira pravañcana
vaiṣṇavera pādodaka, sama nahe ei saba,
jāte hoya vāñchita purāṇa

The Puranas have written of the purifying qualities of the water of the holy places, but these are just a deception that lead us away from bhakti. The water from the holy places cannot be compared to that which has washed the feet of a Vaishnava, for only this water can fulfill all one's desires.

vaiṣṇava-saṅgete mana,
ānandita anukṣana,
sadā hoya kṛṣṇa-parasaṅga
dīna narottama kānde,
hiyā dhairya nāhi bāndhe,
more daśā keno hoilo bhaṅga

I am always joyful in the company of Vaishnavas, for they are constantly discussing the topics of Sri Krishna. My heart cannot find peace now that I have been deprived of their companionship, laments Narottam Das.

CHAPTER 7

Following *in the* Footsteps

When Balaram heard that the Pandavas were about to become involved in a war with their cousins, the Kauravas, he did not want to pick sides. To avoid getting caught in the middle of their conflict, He decided to leave Dwaraka, using the pretext of going on a pilgrimage to bathe in various holy places. He thought, "Both Duryodhan and Yudhishthir are my friends. If either of them asks Me to fight on their side, I won't know what to do. It would be better to leave town before any such request comes my way. If I tell everyone that I am going to make a pilgrimage to the Saraswati and Ganges Rivers, they will believe Me. I see no other way of avoiding this quarrel."

With this intention, Balaram gathered a party of Brahmins to accompany Him and set off to Prabhasa Tirtha. Like any other pilgrim, He took a sacramental bath in the holy water and then offered oblations to the gods, sages and forefathers. From there, He and His companions headed upstream along the Saraswati River. One by one, they visited Prithudaka, Bindu Sarovar, Tritakupa, Sudarshan, Vishala, Brahma Tirtha, Chakra Tirtha, and Prachi Saraswati—in short, all the major holy places between Dwaraka and the Doab, the territory between the Ganges and Yamuna Rivers.

Following the Ganges eastward, Balaram and His party arrived at Naimisharanya, which lies on the banks of the Gomati River. There, a large number of sages had gathered to perform a great sacrifice. Naimisharanya is also the place where the Puranas were recited by Romaharshan Suta, and where Suta Goswami would later recite the Srimad Bhagavatam.

At the beginning of the Bhagavatam, after uttering the invocatory syllable Om, Vyasa Deva writes—

naimiṣe'nimiṣa-kṣetre
ṛṣayaḥ śaunakādayaḥ
satraṁ svargāya lokāya
sahasra-samam āsata

> In Naimisharanya, the sacred land of Vishnu, the sages headed by Shaunaka had begun the performance of a sacrifice that was to last a thousand years, in the hope of attaining the Lord's abode.
>
> *SB 1.1.4*

Sridhar Swami comments on this verse in his *Bhāvārtha-dīpikā* commentary by first quoting a verse from the Smritis that states that Om and *atha* were the first sounds emitted by Lord Brahma at the beginning of creation. Both are thus very auspicious and should be uttered before starting any work. Furthermore, the appearance of Om at the very beginning of the Srimad Bhagavatam indicates that its goal is to explain this core syllable of the Vedic literatures.

Sridhar Swami then goes on to give information about Naimisharanya taken from the Puranas. The *Vāyu-purāṇa* tells us that some sages once requested Lord Brahma to give them a place that would be safe for performing austerities. Lord Brahma said, "I will create a discus from my mind and throw it. The place where its rim (*nemi*) touches the ground will be auspicious for performing austerities." After saying this, the grandfather of the universe produced from his mind a discus weapon, shining as brilliantly as the sun. After prostrating himself before Lord Shiva, he let the discus fly. The sages joyfully bowed down to Lord Brahma and followed the whirling discus to the place where its rim touched the ground and was bent. The forest surrounding this spot, which was honored as a holy place by all the sages, was thenceforth known as Naimisharanya, "the forest where the rim was bent."

THE SRIMAD BHAGAVATAM, WHICH IS FULL OF THIS TYPE OF POETRY, IS IN FACT THE RIPENED FRUIT OF ALL THE VEDIC SCRIPTURES. WHEN SPOKEN BY A PURE DEVOTEE, THE TOUCH OF HIS LIPS MAKES IT EVEN MORE DELICIOUS.

The sages saw the beauty of the place and recognized it as one where they would be able to fully appreciate the Srimad Bhagavatam and meditate on its meaning.

Srila Bhaktisiddhanta Saraswati interprets this story in the following way:

"Human beings have limited powers of sense perception. They can never understand God with their limited senses, any more than they can reach His abode in their material bodies. Here, the discus produced from Lord Brahma's mind represents the limited knowledge produced from our mundane senses. Naimisha is the name given to the place where such knowledge shatters or becomes aware of its incompetence to reach the transcendental realm described in the Srimad Bhagavatam, for only when one has been thus humbled can one assimilate the Bhagavatam's teachings."

Vivrti 1.1.4

Poems written in glorification of the transcendental Lord's name, qualities and pastimes are also transcendental. The Srimad Bhagavatam, which is full of this type of poetry, is in fact the ripened fruit of all the Vedic scriptures. When spoken by a pure devotee, the touch of his lips makes it even more delicious. When the words about Krishna enter the ears of a devotee whose heart has been prepared by service and the desire to hear, they descend into his very being, touching his heart and causing an emotional revolution. Once this transformation has taken place, the devotee starts to hanker for Krishna. He calls out to Him and eagerly follows the devotional path leading to Vrindavan. On the other hand, the Srimad Bhagavatam, the essence of all the Vedanta, is not accessible to someone who has become puffed up from the acquisition of empirical knowledge arising from material sense perceptions, because its nectarean topics, the persons who distribute them, and the place where they are discussed are all spiritual and beyond the scope of matter.

The word Naimisha is sometimes spelt differently, with a cerebral (ṣ) rather than a palatal sh sound (ś). This spelling means that the word has a different etymology, being derived from the word *nimiṣa*, which means the "blink of an eye." In the *Varāha-purāṇa*, the Lord explains to Gauramukh Rishi that this forest was given the name Naimisharanya because the gods defeated the demon army there in the mere blink of an eye.

Desires for enjoying material sense gratification are the chief danger or enemy on the spiritual path, yet such desires can be destroyed in a wink simply by attentively hearing topics related to Krishna in a holy place. Knowing this, the sages chose Naimisharanya as the ideal place to engage in the service of the Lord, taking a vow to engage in a sacrifice there that was to last a thousand years.

One day, while the sages were engaged in this sacrificial performance, Balaram suddenly appeared in their midst. When they saw Him, they stood up without any hesitation, their hands folded in a gesture of greeting and respect, and then offered Him a seat in accordance with the proper etiquette. Balaram was pleased by the welcome He received, but noticed that one prominent individual, Romaharshan, had not had the good grace to make any show of courtesy whatsoever. Romaharshan was a disciple of Vyasa Deva, and had been given the responsibility of preaching the Puranas by his spiritual master. Although he was seated on the speaker's throne for that purpose, his failure to show respect to the Supreme Lord in the person of Balaram showed that he was unsuited for such a place of honor.

Balaram was not impressed with Romaharshan's behavior and made the following considerations: "Romaharshan has taken birth in a mixed caste. He is a *sūta*, which means he was born of a Brahmin mother and Kshatriya father. It is thus very bad manners on his part to remain on a lofty seat before Me, for I have descended into this world as the protector of religion. All these Brahmin sages, who are members of the noble Bhrigu clan, have shown the proper etiquette by standing up, so why does not he, who is of a lower caste? He may well be Vyasa Deva's student and highly learned; nevertheless, he shows that he has not developed the humility and self-mastery that one would normally expect from someone as educated. Indeed, he seems to have been affected by false pride in his scholarship. I think that all his knowledge of the traditional lore of the epics and Puranic literature is like the memorized dialogue of an actor on stage. It thus cannot have any long-term beneficial effect on those who hear from him. It may be useful as a way of making a livelihood, but other than this personal benefit to him, it does not seem to be of any value whatsoever. Such offensiveness should be punished. I have appeared to rid the world of hypocrites like this, so I shall make an example of him. Those who make an artificial show of religion are far worse than those who are openly sinful while engaged in irreligious life, for they are ultimately the cause of even more sinfulness in this world."

After coming to this conclusion, Baladeva approached Romaharshan's seat. As he did so, he picked a blade of long kusha grass and used its sharp tip to pierce the scholar, putting an end to his life.

Baladeva was on pilgrimage, so He was in fact taking a break from His mission of destroying evil demons and such. Nevertheless, as He had fortuitously come upon someone who fit the description of an asadhu, He gave him the ultimate punishment. The Bhagavata verse says *bhāvitvāt*—it was Romaharshan's fate to die at the hand of the Supreme Lord and therefore inevitable, as no one can avoid their destiny.

The sages were shocked by Balaram's actions and began to lament. Nevertheless, they knew His identity and so, despite their disapproval, spoke to Him in measured tones: "O Lord! What You have done is most improper. We had placed Romaharshan on the elevated seat, known as the seat of Lord Brahma, the original speaker of the Vedic knowledge. Through this, we had conferred on him the status of a Brahmin. We had further blessed him with long life and good health for the duration of the sacrifice so that he would be able to recite the Puranic lore to us without experiencing bodily fatigue. You obviously did not know these things and so committed the sin of killing a Brahmin. O purifier of the world! Even though You are the master of all yoga and the Vedic injunctions do not apply to You, You should still perform some kind of atonement to set an example for the people of this world. Otherwise they will think that You are condoning the indiscriminate performance of great crimes like this."

Baledeva humbly answered them, "My dear sages, I will do as you ask. I shall set an example by atoning for having killed a Brahmin, but please instruct Me how I should go about it. I will do whatever you tell Me. If you tell Me exactly what kinds of blessings of long life, good health and extraordinary ability you had bestowed on Romaharshan, I shall immediately put them back into effect by reviving him with My mystic powers."

The Rishis answered, "You are a valorous warrior. Furthermore, Your use of the kusha grass weapon to kill Romaharshan is an act of truth that cannot be changed. We do not, therefore, ask You to resuscitate him. At the same time, the blessings we gave Romaharshan were a promise that should not have been broken. Please find a way that our promise may be kept without taking back Your deed."

Balaram then said, "O sages! It is said that a man's soul lives on in his son. Therefore, you should replace Romaharshan with his son, Ugrashrava. Place him on the speaker's chair and bless him with all the same gifts of long life, sharp intelligence and the other virtues you gave his father, so that he will be able to carry out all his father's duties. That way your word will be kept. Now as far as I am concerned, please think about what I should do that I may be delivered from the sin of killing a Brahmin. What penance should I perform to atone for this sin?"

On hearing this, the Rishis told Balaram about a wicked demon named Balvala who had been disturbing their sacrifice. They asked Him to protect them from this demon and then to continue His pilgrimage around India for a full year.

Lord Balaram is Vishnu tattva. No sin could possibly touch Him. As such, there was really no need for Him to perform any atonement. Nevertheless, He carried out the directives of the Rishis, atoning for the sin of killing a Brahmin in the way recommended in the Vedic literature. He did so only in order to set an example for human society.

Lord Balaram had no tolerance for religious hypocrisy. Even though Romaharshan was a direct disciple of Vyasa Deva and greatly learned, he was so falsely proud of his learning and so lacking in humility and self-control that he refused to offer respect to Balaram, the defender of righteousness. One will never profit by hearing the Srimad Bhagavatam from the lips of an insolent speaker such as this. Balaram thus stepped in and punished him in order to set the standard of respect for religion.

Those who make an artificial show of religion are far worse than those who are openly sinful

In his poem called "Instructions to My Mind," Raghunath Das Goswami teaches all would-be Vaishnavas and servants of the Lord to give up all arrogance and show humility and respect to the spiritual master, the residents of Vrindavan, the Vaishnavas and the Brahmins:

gurau goṣṭhe goṣṭhā-
layiṣu sujane bhū-sura-gaṇe
sva-mantre śrī-nāmni
vraja-nava-yuva-dvandva-smaraṇe
sadā dambhaṁ hitvā
kuru ratim apūrvām atitarām
aye svāntar bhrātaś
caṭubhir abhiyāce dhṛta-padaḥ

O my mind! My brother! I fall down at your feet and plead with you to give up your insolent attitude and show unparalleled affection for the spiritual master, for Vrindavan and all those who live there, for the devotees and the Brahmins, for the Holy Name, and for remembering the pastimes of the ever-youthful Divine Couple, Radha and Krishna. *Manaḥ-śikṣā 1*

BALARAM *and the* SIEGE *of* HASTINAPUR

Elsewhere in the Bhagavatam (10.68), another story is told about Balaram. Once Samba, the great warrior son of Krishna and Jambavati, abducted Duryodhan's daughter Lakshmana while she was choosing a husband from amongst a number of candidates at her swayamvara ceremony. Since Samba had not been invited, he was immediately attacked by the leading knights of Duryodhan's army, and fought bravely before finally being taken prisoner. When King Ugrasen and the Yadu clan in Dwaraka heard news of these events from Narada Muni, they decided to retaliate and gathered an army to march on Hastinapur. Though Balaram was a member of the Yadu family, He was also Duryodhan's friend. In an attempt to mediate and forestall the imminent hostilities, He went to Hastinapur with a group of Brahmins and respected Yadu elders.

On arriving at Hastinapur, Balaram and His party waited outside the city while Uddhava, one of the Yadavas' most important ministers, went to announce their arrival to King Dhritarashtra. The Kauravas treated Uddhava with great respect and followed him outside to greet Balaram, offering Him the most dignified welcome. After they had inquired into each others' health and well-being, Balaram gave Ugrasen's ultimatum to the Kauravas in a straightforward manner and without false humility. He said, "You have attacked and captured Samba in an unfair fight, since he was alone while you were many in number. Though we consider this to be highly improper, we have decided to overlook the offense in the interest of preserving the friendship between our families. Please show your good faith by turning Samba over to us immediately."

Forgetting who Balaram was, Duryodhan became very impertinent. He said, "It is most astonishing that the Yadavas would give such an ultimatum to the scions of the Kuru dynasty. It is as though the shoes are now vying with the crown for a place on the king's head! This is how time shows its inexorable influence! Because of the relationship forged between our families through the marriage of Pandu with the Yadu princess Kunti, the Yadavas have become very close to us. They eat with us at the same table; they are guests in our house and sleep in our rooms. But now this familiarity has turned to contempt. We have generously permitted them to rule over a part of our empire, to enjoy the privileges of the royal station and use its symbols, but like a snake that bites the very person who feeds it milk, they have turned against us. Though they have been elevated to their position through our blessings, they now think that they can order us around as if they were the lords and we the servants. We think, therefore, that we should repeal their titles and territorial rights. If they wish to do battle with us, they should remember that Indra himself could not take away a kingdom protected by the likes of Bhishma and Drona. The Yadus could not do so any more than a sheep could steal the possessions of a lion."

It is Balaram's nature to become angry with offenders, but He is quick to give up His anger when supplicated.

Puffed up with his royal birth and temporal power and looking to his gallery of sycophants, Duryodhan finished his insulting speech, turned away from Balaram and His party, and went back into his palace.

Balaram was astonished by the impolite behavior of the Kauravas and gave a scornful laugh. He said—

nūnaṁ nānā-madonnaddhāḥ
śāntiṁ necchanty asādhavaḥ
teṣāṁ hi praśamo daṇḍaḥ
paśūnāṁ laguḍo yathā

> "The impious are so obsessed with their selfish concerns that they do not truly desire peace. There is only one way to control such people and that is by force, just as the stick is the only way to deal with animals." *SB 10.68.31*

Balaram continued to review the situation: "I came here because Krishna was angry and the Yadavas were ready to fight. I pacified them and told them to be patient while I came and talked things over with the Kauravas. However, it appears that Duryodhan and his advisors are lacking in good faith and would prefer to fight. Even though I came here only out of a concern for their welfare, they are so arrogant and foolish that they have shown Me disrespect by taunting Me.

"Lord Krishna went to the heavenly kingdom and attacked the assembly-house of the gods, the Sudharma. He took the parijata tree and planted it in His garden in Dwaraka, but they say He is unfit to be king. Though the goddess of fortune serves Krishna's feet constantly, they say He is unworthy of the regal symbols. They don't realize that He is fully able to seize these symbols if that is His wish! But what is the meaning of a worldly crown to Krishna, the dust of whose feet is sought by Indra and the gods and placed on their heads as holier than the holiest of holy waters from the purest of pilgrimage places? We Yadavas rule our kingdom in order to favor the Kauravas, and now they compare themselves to the head and us to the feet? This insult is intolerable! Today I shall free the earth of this burden known as the Kauravas!"

With these words, Balaram, who is also called Haladhar because He uses the plough as a weapon, began to dig up the ground by the city's southern walls, facing the Ganges River. His intention was to drag the entire city of Hastinapur—with the exception of the captive Samba—into the Ganges and submerge it. As the furrows dug by Balaram became deeper and deeper, the city began to shake like a boat buffeted by a storm at sea. When the Kauravas saw that their city was in imminent danger of being pulled into the water, they cried out to Balaram to be merciful and stop. With folded hands, they apologized to Him and spoke words in praise of His great power and glory. Lord Balaram was quickly pacified and told them to have no fear.

It is Balaram's nature to become angry with offenders, but He is quick to give up His anger when supplicated. In His appearance as Nityananda Prabhu, He was also very quick to show mercy to those who surrendered to Him:

preme matta nityānanda kṛpā avatāra
je āge paḍaye tāre karaye nistāra

> Nityananda, the incarnation of mercy, was always intoxicated by love of God. He delivers whoever is first to fall before Him. *CC 1.5.208*

Duryodhan dearly loved his daughter Lakshmana. Now obliged to accept her marriage to Samba, he showered him with many gifts—1,200 young elephants, 10,000 horses, 6,000 chariots decorated with gold filigree, and a thousand female servants adorned

with golden jewelry. Baladeva accepted these wedding gifts on behalf of His nephew and returned to Dwaraka with the newlyweds. To this day, a ridge stands on the southern side of the city of Hastinapur as a testimony to Balaram's great exploit.

Hear *the* Bhagavatam *from the* Lips *of a* Devotee

In the Bhagavad Gita, Lord Krishna calls *dambha*, or hypocrisy, a demonic quality:

dambho darpo'bhimānaś ca
krodhaḥ pāruṣyam eva ca
ajñānaṁ cābhijātasya
pārtha sampadam āsurīm

> O son of Pritha! Hypocrisy, arrogance, the desire for praise, wrath, cruelty and insensitivity to spiritual values—all these are the inheritance of those with demonic tendencies. *Gita 16.4*

Vishwanath Chakravarti explains the word *dambha* as *svasyādharmikatve'pi dhārmikatva-prakhyāpanam*—"advertising oneself as righteous when one is not." This is otherwise known as hypocrisy. The other demonic qualities mentioned in the verse are *darpa*—pride in one's wealth and learning, *abhimāna*—the desire to be praised and honored by others or a deep attachment to one's wife, family and children; *krodha* or anger; *pāruṣya* or cruelty; and *ajñāna* or lack of discrimination. All of these, according to Vishwanath, are signs not only of demons (asuras), or those who are dominated by the modes of passion, but also of the even more evil rakshasas, who are deeply immersed in the mode of ignorance.

These qualities of the demonic nature are what bind the living beings to this world. A proud, conceited hypocrite cannot speak the Bhagavatam or explain its true meaning. No matter how learned such persons are in the scriptures, no one can be genuinely benefited by hearing the Bhagavatam from their lips. Therefore Baladeva, who descended to this world to establish and protect the principles of religion, removed Romaharshan from the seat of the speaker and replaced him with his son, the great Vaishnava named Ugrashrava Suta. Lord Balaram is the spiritual master of the universe. When He placed Ugrashrava on the speaker's seat, He empowered him to expound on the Srimad Bhagavatam and destroy the doubts that filled the hearts of the sages; he alone was competent to fully answer the six questions that they asked him at the beginning of his recital.

As Ugrashrava started speaking the Bhagavatam, he first paid his obeisances to his teacher, Shukadeva. At its end, he again showed his respect with the following verse:

ahaṁ ca saṁsmārita ātma-tattvaṁ
śrutaṁ purā me paramarṣi-vaktrāt
prāyopaveśe nṛpateḥ parīkṣitaḥ
sadasy ṛṣīṇāṁ mahatāṁ ca śṛṇvatām

> "You have so kindly blessed me by reminding me of all those spiritual truths that I first heard when I sat in the assembly with hundreds of other great sages and saints, and Shukadeva Goswami spoke to Maharaj Parikshit while he fasted to the death." *SB 12.12.57*

Ugrashrava, or Suta Goswami, recited the Srimad Bhagavatam just as he had heard Shukadeva speak it to the sixty thousand sages at Naimisharanya, all of whom were firmly devoted to Narayan, the indwelling Supersoul of all creation, the master of the universe, God of all gods and the one worshipable Lord of all. All the four great acharyas—Sri Madhvacharya, Ramanujacharya, Vishnuswami and Nimbarka—and Lord Chaitanya Mahaprabhu Himself—accepted the Srimad Bhagavatam as the essence of all scriptures and the most authoritative source of divine knowledge. The six Goswamis, Lord Chaitanya's dearest associates, made the Srimad Bhagavatam the foundation of their philosophy and the inspiration for their poetic and dramatic works. The Supreme Lord Hari, who destroys all the ills of this Age of Kali, is glorified from the beginning to the end of this Srimad Bhagavatam. Anyone who daily studies the Srimad Bhagavatam intently with faith—whether it be a single verse, a chapter, or even a footnote—will be purified. The Bhagavatam is the divine incarnation in the form of sound, giving transcendental knowledge to those who have been bereft of vision in this age of darkness. From beginning to end, the Bhagavatam glorifies both Krishna and His devotees.

Devananda Pandit

Sri Chaitanya Mahaprabhu also stressed the importance of hearing the Bhagavata from a devotee. Devananda was a famous speaker on the Bhagavatam in Nabadwip, nevertheless Mahaprabhu asked, "What authority does this fellow have to lecture on the Bhagavatam? (*ei beṭāra bhāgavate kon adhikāra*?)" He was so upset that He was about to snatch the manuscript of the Bhagavatam from Devananda before being stopped by his companions. Srila Vrindavan Das Thakur quotes the angry words Mahaprabhu spoke when He heard that Devananda Pandit was lecturing on the Srimad Bhagavatam:

> What right does this fool have to speak on the Bhagavatam? The Srimad Bhagavatam is the literary incarnation of Lord Krishna. According to it, devotional service to the Supreme Lord is the highest perfection of life. The four Vedas say that the Bhagavatam is the embodiment of love for Krishna.
>
> The four Vedas are likened to cream. The Srimad Bhagavatam is the butter that is churned from that cream. Shukadeva is the one who did the churning, while Parikshit Maharaj is the one who relished the finished product. Shukadeva is very dear to Me and fully conversant with the Bhagavatam, and he has described everything about Me there in a way that I fully approve. Anyone who draws a distinction between My servant, the book Bhagavatam and Myself will be lost forever.
>
> Whoever recites the Bhagavatam without glorifying devotional service is an ignorant fool who knows nothing. All the scriptures admit that the Bhagavatam is inconceivable and cannot be understood through material learning, penance or personal power.
>
> Anyone who thinks that he has understood the meaning of the Srimad Bhagavatam will never truly be able to understand it. On the other hand, one who recognizes that the Bhagavatam is the incarnation of the inconceivable Supreme Lord will understand that devotional service is its essential meaning. Though Devananda Pandit is a rare scholar, learned and full of many good qualities, he has misunderstood the Bhagavatam because of his pride and will be punished by Yamaraj, who judges all after death.
>
> *Cbh 2.21. 14-18, 20, 23-27*

In the *Anubhāṣya* to Chaitanya Charitamrita 1.10.77, Srila Bhaktisiddhanta Saraswati gives a brief summary of the events that led to Lord Chaitanya's displeasure with Devananda—

> *sārvabhauma pitā viśārada maheśvara*
> *tāṅhāra jāṅgāle gelā prabhu viśvambhara*
> *sei khāne devānanda paṇḍitera vāsa*
> *parama suśānta vipra mokṣa abhilāṣa*

> One day Sri Chaitanya Mahaprabhu went for a walk near the home of Sarvabhauma Bhattacharya's father, Maheshwar Visharad. Devananda Pandit, a very peaceful Brahmin whose goal in life was to achieve liberation, also made his home nearby. *CC 2.21.6-7*

Devananda lectured on the Bhagavatam, but his goal was to achieve liberation. One day, Srivas Pandit was sitting in the audience as he gave his discourse. On hearing a particularly beautiful description of Lord Krishna, Srivas started to cry in loving ecstasy. Some of Devananda's ignorant students considered this a disruption and began to beat Srivas in order to silence him, but when he continued to cry, they dragged him out of the assembly. Some time later, when Mahaprabhu was passing by Devananda's house, He remembered the indignities suffered by Srivas and became angry, asking what right a faithless person like Devananda had to speak on the Bhagavatam.

Mahaprabhu showed kindness to Devananda a few years later when He passed through his home village of Kuliya on the way to Vrindavan—*kuliyā grāme kaila devānandere prasāda* (CC 2.1.153). Devananda had no faith in Mahaprabhu's divinity, but due to some unseen good fortune, he came into contact with Vakreshwar Pandit. His heart changed when he saw Vakreshwar dance and sing the names of the Lord. Thus, by the mercy of the Lord's devotee, he started to believe in Lord Chaitanya. When Devananda met Mahaprabhu, the Lord instructed him to continue speaking on the Bhagavatam, but to explain it in a way that would lead everyone to devotion. Therefore it is stated:

> *bhāgavatī devānanda*
> *vakreśvara kṛpāte*
> *bhāgavatera bhakti artha*
> *pāila prabhu haite*

> Devananda was a scholar of the Bhagavatam, but it was only through the mercy of Vakreshwar that he was able to understand its meaning from Mahaprabhu.
> *CC 1.10.77*

We can thus conclude that no matter how scholarly someone is according to purely academic standards, if he is not devoted to Krishna, then simply memorizing a few verses is insufficient qualification to speak the glories of the Bhagavatam.

STUDY *the* BHAGAVATAM *with a* VAISHNAVA

Swarup Damodar told the East Bengali Brahmin—

> *jāha bhāgavata paṛa vaiṣṇavera sthāne*
> *ekānta āśraya kara caitanya-caraṇe*
> *caitanya bhakta-gaṇera nitya kara saṅga*
> *tabe ta jānibe siddhānta-samudra-taraṅga*
> *tabe pāṇḍitya tomāra haibe saphala*
> *kṛṣṇera svarūpa-līlā varṇibā nirmala*

> Go and study the Bhagavatam from a Vaishnava. Take exclusive shelter of Chaitanya Mahaprabhu's lotus feet. Always associate with Chaitanya Mahaprabhu's devotees. If you do all this, you will be able to plunge into the ocean of His divine teachings. This will bring your scholarship to fruition and then you will be able to describe Krishna's nature and pastimes purely. *CC 3.5.131-3*

THE FRUIT OF HEARING THE SRIMAD BHAGAVATAM IS THE SERVICE OF LORD KRISHNA. HOWEVER, THIS RESULT WILL NOT MANIFEST IF ONE HEARS FROM A MAYAVADI PHILOSOPHER.

To these verses, our venerable spiritual master Srila Bhaktisiddhanta Saraswati Prabhupada adds the following comments: "The fruit of hearing the Srimad Bhagavatam is the service of Lord Krishna. However, this result will not manifest if one hears from a Mayavadi philosopher who is dedicated to the undifferentiated monistic unity, nor if one hears from the clever but devotionless lexical and grammatical scholar, nor from the hedonist who seeks to find many exciting new interpretations of the text. Hearing the Srimad Bhagavatam from such persons will not have a purifying effect, but rather will cause further entanglement in the sufferings and enjoyments of material life. One must study the Bhagavatam from a detached Vaishnava on the highest platform of spiritual achievement. The greatest treasure for the aspiring devotee is the understanding of the Bhagavatam as given by someone who has made Lord Chaitanya's lotus feet his only shelter. The devotees of Lord Chaitanya are His eternal associates. They alone know the transcendental truths of spiritual life. One who can remain constantly in their association becomes free of material ignorance and sees the divine conclusions of the scriptures as they are."

Anubhāṣya 3.5.131-132

Sometimes those who have no devotion to the Lord may still dress like Vaishnavas, putting on tilak and neck beads just to make money from lecturing. Such persons not only suffer the consequences of their hypocrisy themselves, but all who hear from them are also doomed.

śāstra paṛāiyā sabe ei karma kare
śrotāra sahita yama-pāśe ḍubi mare

> Though they teach the scripture, they engage in all these other activities; both they and their students end up caught in the snares of Yamaraj. *Cbh 1.2.68*

The following verse is found in the *Atri-saṁhitā:*

vedair vihīnāś ca paṭhanti śāstraṁ
śāstreṇa hīnāś ca purāṇa-pāṭhāḥ
purāṇa-hīnāḥ kṛṣiṇo bhavanti
bhraṣṭās tato bhāgavatā bhavanti

> Unworthy Brahmins who are unable to understand the Vedas turn to the study of the Dharma Shastras. Those who are unable to understand such scriptures then turn to the study of the Puranas. Those who cannot understand the Puranas end up as tillers of the soil. Even so, such fallen Brahmins still think they can speak on the Bhagavatam!

Such persons are called false Vaishnavas, for they think that the Bhagavatam is just another tool for commerce, an item to sell. They thus get the very bad idea of making a living by putting on performances of the Bhagavatam, turning it into some kind of entertainment. But the Bhagavatam itself clearly warns: *na vyākhyām upayuñjīta*—"Don't make a living by explaining the scriptures." (SB 7.13.8) The *Brahma-vaivarta-purāṇa* also says—

yo harer nāma-vikrayī
yo vidyā-vikrayī vipro
viṣa-hīno yathoragaḥ

> The Brahmin who sells the names of the Lord or one who sells his knowledge is as ineffectual as a snake without venom.

The Bhagavatam heard from such a person may provide a few moments of entertainment, but it will not be of much help in achieving the ultimate goal of human life. The book Bhagavatam must be heard from the person Bhagavata—the person who has assimilated the Srimad Bhagavatam fully into his own thought, word and deed.

dui bhāi hṛdayera kṣāli andhakāra
dui bhāgavata saṅge karān sākṣātkāra
eka bhāgavata baḍa bhāgavata śāstra
āra bhāgavata bhakta bhakti-rasa-pātra
dui bhāgavata-dvārā diyā bhakti-rasa
tāṅhāra hṛdaye tāṅra preme haya vaśa

> The two brothers, Gaura and Nitai, wash away the darkness in our hearts by means of the two Bhagavatas to which they have introduced us. The first of the Bhagavatas is very important—it is the scripture of that name. The second Bhagavata is the devotee of the Lord, who relishes the acts of devotion. Gauranga and Nityananda give a taste of bhakti to the devotional aspirant through these two Bhagavatas and then, when the aspirant attains love for Them, They become bound up in his or her heart. *CC 1.1.98-100*

One must study the book Bhagavatam through the medium of the devotee Bhagavata to attain pure devotional service to Krishna. Only when we practice pure devotion will we achieve love for Krishna, or prema. Sri Sri Gauranga and Nityananda are conquered by such love. Therefore it is said in the Bhagavatam—

yasyāṁ vai śrūyamāṇāyāṁ
kṛṣṇe parama-pūruṣe
bhaktir utpadyate puṁsaḥ
śoka-moha-bhayāpahā

> By hearing the Srimad Bhagavatam from the devotee Bhagavata, one is blessed with devotion to Krishna, the Supreme Personality of Godhead. The awakening of devotion results in the termination of all grief, bewilderment and fear. *SB 1.7.7*

CHAPTER 8

The Blessings *of the* Great Devotee

When Shaunaka Rishi and the sixty thousand scions of the Bhrigu dynasty began listening to the sweet recitation of the Bhagavatam from the lips of the great devotee, Ugrashrava, they wished to show their appreciation and eagerness to hear more. They blessed him with the words, "May you live forever." As a result of hearing from him, their feelings of devotion for Krishna had grown so much that they had come to realize the worthlessness of the path of ritual actions. They said,

karmaṇy asminn anāśvāse
dhūma-dhūmrātmanāṁ bhavān
āpāyayati govinda-
pāda-padmāsavaṁ madhu

"We had been engaged in this sacrifice until our bodies were blackened by smoke, and yet were uncertain of its benefits because of the unknown effects of imperfections in its performance. But now you have come and revitalized us by giving the honey nectar from Govinda's lotus feet to drink." *SB 1.18.12*

In their gratitude they continued,

tulayāma lavenāpi
na svargaṁ nāpunar-bhavam
bhagavat-saṅgi-saṅgasya
martyānāṁ kim utāśiṣaḥ

"We cannot compare even the briefest moment of association with the companions of the Lord to heaven or liberation. If this is so, then how can we compare it to the miserable benedictions that come to the worldly from mundane religious ritual activities?" *SB 1.18.13; CC 2.22.55*

The rishis considered the association of devotees who had come into contact with the Lord even more desirable, praiseworthy, and worshipable than association with the Lord Himself. No wonder, when the result of hearing about Krishna from the pure devotee is that all mundane desires for sense pleasure, liberation or mystic power evaporate like mist. Such is the glory of Krishna's virtues.

Thus Krishna Das Kaviraj glorifies the association of devotees—

sādhu saṅga sādhu saṅga sarva śāstra kaya
lava-mātra sādhu saṅge sarva siddhi haya

All the scriptures glorify the association of devotees, again and again. Just a moment's association with the devotees results in all perfection. *CC 2.22.54*

Materialists seek gross sense enjoyment in this life and the next; when seeking subtle sense enjoyment, they look for liberation, yogic perfection and mystic powers. The devotee who has come to understand and experience the glories of devotion considers all these things to be without value or useless. The only thing with real meaning for him is deep and intense love for Krishna. Such a person merits the title of mahat. Unless one takes shelter of such a devotee's lotus feet, one cannot even be liberated from one's entanglements, what to speak of attaining love for Krishna.

mahat-kṛpā vinā kono karme bhakti naya
kṛṣṇa-bhakti dūre rahu, saṁsāra nahe kṣaya

Without the favor of a great devotee, no activity qualifies as devotion. Not only is one unable to attain pure devotion to Krishna, but one cannot even be freed from the bondage of material existence. *CC 2.22.51*

The great devotee Prahlada said something similar to Hiranyakashipu—

naiṣāṁ matis tāvad urukramāṅghriṁ
spṛśaty anarthāpagamo yad-arthaḥ
mahīyasāṁ pāda-rajo-bhiṣekaṁ
niṣkiñcanānāṁ na vṛṇīta yāvat

The consciousness of materialistic persons never approaches the feet of the glorious Lord, yet only consciousness of His feet can drive away all undesirable things from our hearts. They can never attain such consciousness unless they first smear upon their bodies the dust of the lotus feet of a Vaishnava completely freed from material contamination. *SB 7.5.32*

The mighty king Rishabhadeva described the mahat to his sons before turning over the kingdom to them and taking to the renounced life—

mahat-sevāṁ dvāram āhur vimuktes
tamo-dvāraṁ yoṣitāṁ saṅgi-saṅgam
mahāntas te sama-cittāḥ praśāntā
vimanyavaḥ suhṛdaḥ sādhavo ye

It is said that the gateway to liberation is service to the great souls or mahats, while the door to darkness and ignorance is the association of those who are overly attached to sex. Great souls are those saintly people who are equanimous, peaceful, free from pride and anger and friendly to all creatures. *SB 5.5.2*

The wise are divided into two types: those who worship the impersonal Brahman and those who worship the personal God. Through

serving the great souls or mahats, the former merge into Brahman, while the latter attain the personal association of the Lord in His abode. Both thus recognize the association of the mahats as the gateway to these two kinds of liberation. At the same time, the company of the promiscuous is the gateway to hell and bondage. The primary characteristic of the mahat is his commitment to the Supreme Lord; his secondary characteristics are his equanimity, his freedom from anger, his engagement in welfare work for all creatures and his reluctance to find fault with anyone.

ye vā mayīśe kṛta-sauhṛdārthā
janeṣu dehambhara-vārtikeṣu
gṛheṣu jāyātmaja-rātimatsu
na prīti-yuktā yāvad-arthāś ca loke

Those who have established a feeling of friendliness toward Me, the Supreme Lord, and consider My love to be the most important thing in their lives, who think that nothing else in life is as meaningful, who have no interest in mingling with people who are simply engaged in maintaining their bodies, who are themselves not attached to home, wife, children, friends or wealth, and who do not seek more than they need to keep body and soul together, are worthy of the name mahat. *SB 5.5.3*

This exclusive love for the Supreme Lord is the singular characteristic of the mahat. It is possible to attain pure devotion to the Lord only through the mercy of a pure devotee who possesses the characteristics of a mahat.

What is such pure devotion like? Srila Rupa Goswami gives the fundamental definition of pure devotion in his *Bhakti-rasāmṛta-sindhu*—

anyābhilāṣitā-śūnyaṁ
jñāna-karmādy-anāvṛtam
ānukūlyena kṛṣṇānu-
śīlanaṁ bhaktir uttamā

The highest category of devotion or bhakti is defined as the culture of service to Krishna in a way that is most pleasing to Him, devoid of all material desires such as that for illicit sex or other immoral activities, unadulterated by monistic philosophy or fruitive action.
BRS 1.1.11

In this verse, the secondary characteristics of devotional service are given first. This is the avoidance of all things that act against developing love for Krishna, such as jnana and karma. Jnana means the cultivation of knowledge leading to liberation, but not the attempt to understand sambandha, abhidheya and prayojana tattvas. Similarly the karma that is to be avoided refers to the rituals and other regular and occasional religious duties enjoined in the Smritis, and not to the activities of devotional service like worshiping the Lord's deity form and rendering service to the guru and the Vaishnavas. The word *ādi* refers to other spiritual activities that are similarly unhelpful to the attainment of Krishna consciousness.

The best kind of such culture is in the nine types of devotional service described in the Srimad Bhagavatam. Practice of such devotional service is done exclusively for the pleasure of Krishna and leads to divine love for the Lord.

Therefore, Krishna Das Kaviraj Goswami writes,

anya vāñchā anya pūjā chāḍi jñāna karma
ānukūlye sarvendriye kṛṣṇānuśīlana
ei śuddha bhakti ihā haite prema haya
pañcarātre bhāgavate ei lakṣaṇa kaya

Both the Pancharatra and the Bhagavatam describe pure devotional service as the engagement of all the senses in the favorable cultivation of Krishna consciousness, abandoning all other desires and all other worshipable objects, giving up ritualistic religious practices

> or philosophical speculation. Through such pure devotion, one attains prema.
> *CC 2.19.168-169*

In the Srimad Bhagavatam, the following verses are found:

> *sālokya-sārṣṭi-sāmīpya-*
> *sārūpyaikatvam apy uta*
> *dīyamānaṁ na gṛhṇanti*
> *vinā mat-sevanaṁ janāḥ*
>
> *sa eva bhakti-yogākhya*
> *ātyantika udāhṛtaḥ*
> *yenātivrajya tri-guṇaṁ*
> *mad-bhāvāyopapadyate*

> Unless he is assured of having service to the Lord, a pure devotee does not accept any kind of liberation, whether it be residence on the same planet, equal opulences to the Lord, proximity to Him, having the same form as the Lord, or monistic union, even though they may be offered by the Lord.
>
> Thus have I described the superlative stage of that which is known as bhakti-yoga. By mastering this discipline, one can overcome the three qualities of material nature and attain true feeling (*bhāva*) for Me. *SB 3.29.12-13*

Srila Vishwanath Chakravarti Thakur explains the word *bhāva* ("feeling") in this verse as love for Krishna. Association with devotees is the source of love for Krishna. Bad association is to be avoided at all costs. The Bhagavata instructs, *tato duḥsaṅgam utsṛjya satsu sajjeta buddhimān*—"the intelligent person eschews the company of the wicked and stays in that of the saintly." Rupa Goswami quotes a verse from the *Kātyāyana-saṁhitā* and another from the *Viṣṇu-rahasya*

to support this principle:

varaṁ huta-vaha-jvālā-
pañjarāntar-vyavasthitiḥ
na śauri-cintā-vimukha-
jana-saṁvāsa-vaiśasam

Better to be locked in a cage surrounded by burning flames than to suffer in the association of those who dislike thinking of Krishna. *Hari-bhakti-vilāsa 10.295*

Jiva Goswami notes in his *Durgama-saṅgaminī* commentary that the word *vaiśasam* means "great danger."

āliṅganaṁ varaṁ manye
vyāla-vyāghra-jalaukasām
na saṅgaḥ śalya-yuktānāṁ
nānā-devaika-sevinām

I believe that it is better to embrace a python, a tiger or a crocodile rather than to be pierced with the dart of associating with the worshiper of many gods.
BRS 1.2.112, from Viṣṇu-rahasya

Here Jiva comments on the word *śalya* ("dart" or "spear"), comparing it to the desire to serve many other gods besides Krishna (*tat-tad-devatāntara-sevā-vāsanā*). He himself uses this word in his *Gopāla-campū,*

nṛpo na hari-sevitā
vyaya-kṛtī na hary-arpakaḥ
kavir na hari-varṇakaḥ
śrita-gurur na hary-āśritaḥ
guṇī na hari-tat-paraḥ
sarala-dhīr na kṛṣṇāśrayaḥ
sa na vraja-rāmānugaḥ
sva-hṛdi sapta śalyāni me

There are seven darts that pierce my heart and give me great pain. They are: the king who does not serve Krishna; the person who has money to spend but offers not a penny to Krishna; the poet who does not use his talent to glorify Krishna; the person who has taken initiation from a spiritual master, but does not take refuge in Krishna; the virtuous person who does not think of Krishna; the person with clear intelligence who has not taken shelter of Krishna; and finally, the one who has taken shelter of Krishna, but does not follow in the footsteps of the gopis.
Gopāla-pūrva-campū 33.61

yasyāsti bhaktir bhagavaty akiñcanā
sarvair guṇais tatra samāsate surāḥ
harāv abhaktasya kuto mahad-guṇā
mano-rathenāsati dhāvato bahiḥ

In one who has devotion for the Supreme Lord without any desire for personal gain, the demigods invest all their qualities, which otherwise result from practicing religious duties, cultivating knowledge or renunciation. As for the one without such devotion, where are his virtues? Overcome by many desires, engaged in religious ritual and the search for empirical knowledge, or attached to house and family, he is bereft of exclusive devotion to Krishna. Being on the mental plane, he is always running after impermanent things in the external existence. How then is it possible for such a person to be truly virtuous? *SB 5.18.12*

The conclusion is, then, that even one who is decorated with all good qualities must sincerely take shelter of a pure devotee and engage fully in the service of the spiritual master, Krishna, and the Vaishnavas, otherwise all such magnificent virtues lose their value.

The devotee thus prays,

sādhu-saṅge kṛṣṇa-nāma ei mātra cāi
saṁsāra jinite āra kono vastu nāi

All I desire is to chant the Holy Name in the company of saintly Vaishnavas. I know of nothing more powerful than this in helping one to cross over the ocean of material existence. *Prema-vivarta 6.13*

Chapter 9

The Qualities *of a* Vaishnava

In the Uddhava Gita of the Eleventh Canto of the Srimad Bhagavatam, where Lord Krishna imparts His teachings to Uddhava, the following exchange is found:

sādhus tavottama-śloka
mataḥ kīdṛg-vidhaḥ prabho
bhaktis tvayy upayujyeta
kīdṛśī sadbhir ādṛtā
etan me puruṣādhyakṣa
lokādhyakṣa jagat-prabho
praṇatāyānuraktāya
prapannāya ca kathyatām

> Uddhava asked, "O Lord! You who are praised with delightful verses! Whom exactly do You consider to be a saintly man, or sadhu? And what kind of devotion to You do such saintly persons particularly prefer? O director of humankind, O director of the universe, O lord of the worlds! Please explain these things to me, for I am prostrated before You, attached to You and surrendered to You alone." *SB 11.11.26-27*

In answer to this, the Lord first lists the twenty-eight qualities of the Vaishnava saint:

kṛpālur akṛta-drohas
titikṣuḥ sarva-dehinām
satya-sāro'navadyātmā
samaḥ sarvopakārakaḥ
kāmair ahata-dhīr dānto
mṛduḥ śucir akiñcanaḥ
anīho mita-bhuk śāntaḥ
sthiro mac-charaṇo muniḥ
apramatto gabhīrātmā
dhṛti māñ jita-ṣaḍ-guṇaḥ
amānī mānadaḥ kalyo
maitraḥ kāruṇikaḥ kaviḥ

Devotees are compassionate (*kṛpālu*), that is, they cannot bear to see anyone suffering in this world. They do not make enemies (*akṛta-droha*), even when others act towards them in an irrationally aggressive manner. They are tolerant (*titikṣu*), meaning that they forgive the offenses of all other creatures, even those who insult them. They are committed to the truth (*satya-sāra*), in other words, they take strength in the truth. They are faultless (*anavadyātmā*), free of flaws like envy, and do not cause a disturbance to the least of God's creatures, whether in word, thought or deed. They are equanimous (*sama*), taking happiness and distress, praise or criticism without being disturbed. They are helpers to all (*sarvopakāraka*), well-wishers of all creatures, and act for their welfare, especially by helping them to understand their constitutional position as spiritual beings. Their intelligence is not disrupted by desire (*kāmair ahata-dhīḥ*). They have control over their external senses (*dāntaḥ*). They are gentle (*mṛdu*), clean (*śuci*) and not accumulative (*akiñcana*). They are indifferent to the four goals in life, including liberation. The devotees are inactive (*anīha*), in the sense that they do not engage in purely mundane activities, whether based in sense gratification or renunciation. Their eating is controlled (*mita-bhuk*), which means not only that they eat a limited amount of pure foodstuffs, but that they only consume what is absolutely necessary. They are peaceful (*śānta*), for as it is said,

kṛṣṇa bhakta niṣkāma ata eva śānta
bhukti mukti siddhi kāmī sakale aśānta

> The devotee of Krishna has no desires and is therefore peaceful. Those who seek sense enjoyment, liberation or mystic perfection, all lack peace.
> *CC 2.19.149*

The devotees' sense of tranquility (*śama*) comes as a result of their intelligence being fixed in Krishna (*śamo man-niṣṭhatā buddheḥ*, SB 11.19.36). Being peaceful and having the mind fixed on Krishna are synonymous. Devotees are steady (*sthira*); if they take up a service or duty, they see things through to the end without being perturbed. Devotees take exclusive shelter of Krishna (*mac-charaṇa*). They are sage, possessing all the qualities of the *sthita-dhīḥ* described in the second chapter of the Bhagavad Gita. They are careful (*apramatta*): being always fixed in devotional service, they do not become obsessed with material gains or pleasures. They are profound (*gabhīrātmā*): their actions are not always easily understood by others due to their detachment from the customary motivations of ordinary people and their deep meditation on the Lord. They are patient or steady (*dhṛtimān*), meaning that they have conquered over the tongue and genitals, and are capable of distinguishing between the permanent and the impermanent, or good and bad. They have conquered over the six "knots" or "waves" (*jita-ṣaḍ-guṇa*)—hunger, thirst, grief, bewilderment, old age and death. They are humble (*amānī*), seeking no honor for themselves. They are respectful (*mānada*), willing to give all honor to others. They are capable (*kalya*), meaning that they are expert in explaining spiritual matters to others and engaging them in devotional service. They are friendly (*maitra*), which means that they do not cheat others, especially not when it comes to spiritual doctrine. They are merciful (*kāruṇika*), unable to tolerate the sufferings of others, which come as a result of ignorance of spiritual truths. And finally, they are wise (*kavi*)—they know what is liberating and what is entangling.

They are merciful, unable to tolerate the sufferings of others, which come as a result of ignorance of spiritual truths.

Krishna concludes the passage with the following statement:

ājñāyaivaṁ guṇān doṣān
mayādiṣṭān api svakān
dharmān santyajya yaḥ sarvān
māṁ bhajeta sa tu sattamaḥ

> The saintliest of all saints is one who worships Me after giving up his own mundane religious duties, even though they have been enjoined by Me, in full knowledge of their benefits and dangers.
> *SB 11.11.32*

In other words, a devotee who possesses all the above qualities and surrenders to Krishna may give up all the other duties of the Varnashram Dharma that Krishna Himself has enjoined through the medium of the scriptures. He does so after analyzing the risks and benefits that come from such renunciation. On the one hand, he is aware that by surrendering to Krishna all things will be achieved and, on the other, that these other activities are simply a distraction to pure devotional service. One who thus renounces all other duties in order to serve Krishna is considered to be the saintliest of all saints.

Srila Prabhupada Bhaktisiddhanta Saraswati Thakur has commented on these verses in his *Vivṛti*.

> In the first three of these verses, twenty-eight qualities of the Lord's devotees are enumerated. Of these, taking exclusive shelter of Krishna is the most important

(*kṛṣṇaika-śaraṇa*) and the other twenty-seven qualities all depend on this one.

(1) A devotee who has taken exclusive shelter of Krishna is compassionate (*kṛpālu*), and he shows this compassion by distributing the unlimited mercy of Lord Chaitanya Mahaprabhu.

(2) The devotee is *akṛta-droha*: he makes no enemies. The Mayavadi who commits spiritual suicide merits the title, "bewildered by false ego." The fruitive worker is also a kind of spiritual suicide because of his other desires. Being engaged in activities connected to fruitive work, yoga, study, learning, or ignorance, he is not only a spiritual suicide, but also the cause of suffering to others, because he has no knowledge of the real self and his understanding of religion and duty is thus relative. The surrendered devotee is affectionate to all beings. In body, mind and words, he never desires ill for anyone.

(3) The devotee is tolerant (*titikṣu*). In other words, he can bear everything like the earth. He does not lose composure in the face of mundane disturbances. He does not enter into apparently desirable things, even merging into Brahman or the Supersoul, but simply tolerates the misery they cause. He does not engage in activities like eating the flesh and drinking the blood of lower creatures. He generously gives of himself by loudly glorifying the names of the Lord, showing no reserve in the exercise of compassion.

(4) The devotee is committed to the truth (*satya-niṣṭha*). He knows that the one spiritual truth—through past, present and future—is the uninterrupted personification of joy, the enjoyer, and the one worthy object of service. As a result, he does not waste his time in other worthless pursuits.

(5) The devotee is free of flaws like envy (*anavadyātmā*). Because he sees that all things in the universe are knowingly or unknowingly engaged in Krishna's service, he does not cause a disturbance to the least of them, whether in thought, word or deed.

(6) The devotee sees all things equally (*sama-darśī*). Being fixed in the eternal substance, he does not place much importance on the higher and lower states in this world, taking happiness and distress, praise or criticism without being disturbed. He is not influenced or excited by the temporary events that are constantly going on around him, but remains a detached observer.

(7) The devotee is engaged in working for the welfare of the entire world (*sarvopakāraka*). Ordinarily people define welfare work as any personal effort made for the satisfaction of another's senses. The opposite of this is *para-apakāra*, which means to work for one's own sense pleasure at the expense of others'. Welfare work is considered of a higher order depending on the superiority of the object one serves; the ultimate welfare work is therefore service of the Supreme. Krishna is the unique source of all things, material and spiritual. To serve Him and to serve His servants is thus the highest level of welfare activity.

(8) The devotee's intelligence is not disrupted by material desires (*vāsanā-varjita-vicāra-parāyaṇa*). When one is on the platform of resistance to the service of Krishna, then he views all things

and people in the world as utilitarian objects meant for his own pleasure and therefore seeks some sensual payoff from everyone that he encounters. Lord Kamadeva himself becomes the fuel for the fire of one's material desires, though he never reveals himself. He completely envelops the conditioned soul in his illusory power and then shows him temptations and dresses him up in the identity of an enjoyer. The wise soul who has taken exclusive shelter of Krishna is liberated and situated in complete joy; he does not let himself be deceived by the attractions of the material world, no matter how appealing.

The devotee is not attracted by the temptation of sound in the way that a deer becomes hypnotized by beautiful music; nor is he tempted by satisfying odors, nor attached to delicious foodstuffs, nor does he scurry left and right to protect himself from the oppression of excessive heat or cold. The devotee who has taken exclusive shelter of Krishna and dedicated himself entirely to His service recognizes that Krishna is the only enjoyer of all pleasures and desires. He does not permit himself to be led astray by any of the temptations of the world, and thus his intelligence remains calm and undisrupted.

(9) The devotee is self-controlled (*dānta*). He is completely uninterested in engaging the senses in immoral activities as a means of finding happiness. Indeed, he is always on guard against their engagement in anything other than the service of Krishna.

(10) The devotee is gentle (*mṛdu*). The ordinary conditioned soul is constantly being buffeted by enemies who act harshly and cruelly. This distracts and disturbs him and impels him to respond in the same fashion. The devotee is gentle by nature.

(11) The devotee is clean (*śuci*). Impurity and impropriety cannot touch him. Just by remembering the Vaishnava, all of one's sins dissipate, so how can he be anything but pure?

(12) The devotee is not accumulative (*akiñcana*). Our possessions in this world are like shadows, so what value do they have? Why then should we waste our energy chasing after them? One who has taken refuge of Krishna's lotus feet knows that everything in this world is destructible in the course of time and so has no desire to attach himself emotionally by becoming an owner. One who takes a voluntary vow of poverty seeks neither dharma, nor artha, nor kama, nor moksha.

(13) The devotee is inactive (*anīha*), in the sense that he does not engage in any activities based on sense gratification or renunciation. Even so, because of the eternal sense of self, he is fixed in his identity as the Lord's servant, and is thus constantly engaged in His service. Because he is indifferent to the attitudes of the enjoyer and the renouncer, he is always free from the calls of the modes of passion and ignorance.

(14) The devotee has control over his eating (*mita-bhuk*). This means that, in accordance with Rupa Goswami's injunction, he only consumes what is appropriate. He does not consume himself in the fire of sense gratification like the ordinary materialist, but neither does he unnecessarily renounce sense gratification just so that he can attract the praise and admiration of others.

(15) The devotee is peaceful (*śānta*). When disruptions arise from contact with the sense objects, he can detach himself from them, because he is more interested in serving the Lord than in pleasing his senses.

(16) The devotee is steady (*sthira*), his mind unperturbed. Because he is never absorbed

in the not-Krishna, if he takes up any service or duty, he sees things through to the end without ever losing composure.

(17) The devotee takes exclusive shelter of Krishna (*mac-charaṇa*). He has no taste for anything other than Krishna. Firm in his identity as the eternal servant of Krishna, he is always conscious of the service he must perform on behalf of his Lord. He is never swayed by temptations that lead him away from Krishna, nor does he even think that anything can be enjoyed independently of Krishna.

(18) The devotee is sage, possessing all the qualities of the *sthita-dhīḥ* described in the second chapter of the Bhagavad Gita. This means that he is not swayed by the happinesses and distresses of the world, nor does he get carried away by passionate desires or violent hates. Nor does he get angry when his personal plans are disrupted.

> FIRM IN HIS IDENTITY AS THE ETERNAL SERVANT OF KRISHNA, HE IS ALWAYS CONSCIOUS OF THE SERVICE HE MUST PERFORM ON BEHALF OF HIS LORD.

(19) The devotee is careful (*apramatta*): being always fixed in devotional service, he does not forget Krishna and become obsessed with material gains or pleasures.

(20) The devotee is profound (*gabhīrātmā*): he does not let himself get carried away in the waves of the non-self.

(21) The devotee is steadfast or resolute (*dhṛtimān*). This means he is capable of distinguishing between the permanent and impermanent, good or bad.

(22) The devotee has conquered over the six "knots" or "waves" (*jita-ṣaḍ-guṇa*)—hunger, thirst, grief, bewilderment, old age and death.

(23) The devotee is humble (*amānī*), meaning that he cares nothing for mundane honors.

(24) The devotee is respectful (*mānada*), giving all living beings the respect they inherently merit as parts and parcels of the Divine.

(25) The devotee is expert (*kalya*), meaning that he has the capacity to explain spiritual matters and to engage people in devotional service.

(26) The devotee is a friend (*mitra*). He does not deceive anyone, but acts as a friend to all out of a concern for their welfare.

(27) The devotee is compassionate (*kāruṇika*). He proves his inability to tolerate the suffering of others by delivering them from their own foolishness.

(28) And finally, the devotee is a poet (*kavi*). He worships Krishna according to the poetry that has been written about His pastimes. He knows that Krishna's majestic, intimate and beneficent pastimes are not separate from each other, but form a harmonious whole. Thus he does not see any contradictions between them.

There are many sadhus whose devotion is mixed with karma, jnana or yoga, but the truly pure, exclusive devotee is very rare indeed.

ājñāyaivaṁ guṇān doṣān
mayādiṣṭān api svakān
dharmān santyajya yaḥ sarvān
māṁ bhajeta sa tu sattamaḥ

The saintliest of all saints is one who worships Me after giving up his own mundane religious duties, even though they been have enjoined by Me, in full knowledge of the benefits and risks in doing so. *SB 11.11.32*

This verse is about such a pure, exclusive devotee. The topmost sadhu, the pure devotee, knows nothing other than the desire to please Krishna's senses, which bears no direct connection to the satisfaction of his own senses. This is the sadhu that we must seek out if we wish to find the ultimate benefit in life. One who seeks love for God must take refuge in a person who has made the love of God his only treasure.

MORE VAISHNAVA QUALITIES

In the Third Canto of the Srimad Bhagavatam, Lord Kapila Deva instructed his mother Devahuti in the qualifications and characteristics of a pure devotee. He introduces the topic by contrasting the undesirable association of the womanizer with the highly beneficial company of saints:

prasaṅgam ajaraṁ pāśam
ātmanaḥ kavayo viduḥ
sa eva sādhuṣu kṛto
mokṣa-dvāram apāvṛtam

The wise say that attachment to wife and family are a cause of material bondage. If one has the same kind of attachment to saintly devotees, then this will result in the development of detachment and other noble virtues. In such association, the door to liberation is swung open.
SB 3.25.20

Kapila then goes on to describe such a saintly person's characteristics:

titikṣavaḥ kāruṇikāḥ
suhṛdaḥ sarva-dehinām
ajāta-śatravaḥ śāntāḥ
sādhavaḥ sādhu-bhūṣaṇāḥ

Those who are tolerant, merciful and friendly to all creatures, who make no enemies and who are peaceful, are verily jewels amongst the saintly. *SB 3.25.21*

mayy ananyena bhāvena
bhaktiṁ kurvanti ye dṛḍhām
mat-kṛte tyakta-karmāṇas
tyakta-svajana-bāndhavāḥ

With their emotions fixed exclusively in Me, these sadhus engage in staunch devotional service to Me. They renounce all activities as well as friendships and family relationships for My sake. *SB 3.25.22*

mad-āśrayāḥ kathā mṛṣṭāḥ
śṛṇvanti kathayanti ca
tapanti vividhās tāpā
naitān mad-gata-cetasaḥ

Taking shelter of Me, they engage in constantly hearing and chanting about Me. The various kinds of material miseries do not affect them because they are always filled with thoughts of My pastimes and activities. *SB 3.25.23*

ta ete sādhavaḥ sādhvi
sarva-saṅga-vivarjitāḥ
saṅgas teṣv atha te prārthyaḥ
saṅga-doṣa-harā hi te

O virtuous lady! These sadhus are free from all attachment. You should pray for the association of such holy persons, for that will counteract the pernicious effects of contact with the unholy. *SB 3.25.24*

When we hear Krishna's name, form, qualities and pastimes from a sadhu of this quality, we quickly traverse the various levels of devotional practice to attain bhava and then prema.

King Rishabhadeva, before abandoning his throne to his sons, gave them a lengthy homily on the true purpose of life. He told them that when one has taken birth as a human, one who is truly intelligent will awaken to the fact that the mortal body is simply fodder for scavenging animals like vultures and jackals, and therefore recognize that the superficial pleasures of the body are not its goal. Everyone should seek the service of great souls by whom the doors to liberation are opened, rather than the unholy association of the materially attached, who open the three doors to hell—lust, anger and greed.

mahat-sevāṁ dvāram āhur vimuktes
tamo-dvāraṁ yoṣitāṁ saṅgi-saṅgam
mahāntas te sama-cittāḥ praśāntā
vimanyavaḥ suhṛdaḥ sādhavo ye

It is said that the gateway to liberation is service to the great souls or mahats, while the door to darkness and ignorance is the association of those who are overly attached to sex. The great souls are equanimous, peaceful, free from pride and anger, friends to all and fundamentally good people. *SB 5.5.2*

In this verse the qualities of the mahat are again given: equanimity, commitment to the Supreme Lord, freedom from anger, dedication to the welfare of all beings, and freedom from the faultfinding tendency. In the next verse, Rishabhadeva goes on to emphasize the commitment or dedication to the service of the Supreme Lord as the essential characteristic of the mahat:

ye vā mayīśe kṛta-sauhṛdārthā
janeṣu dehambhara-vārtikeṣu
gṛheṣu jāyātmaja-rātimatsu
na prīti-yuktā yāvad-arthāś ca loke

Those who have established a feeling of friendliness toward Me, the Supreme Lord, and consider My love to be the most important thing in their lives, who think that nothing else in life is as important, who have no interest in mingling with people who are simply engaged in maintaining their bodies, who are themselves not attached to homes, wife, children, friends or wealth, and who do not seek more than they need to keep body and soul together are deserving of the epithet "mahat." *SB 5.5.3*

In the first of the above two verses, the general symptoms of the mahat are described, while the second gives a more detailed view of his core characteristics. Of those mentioned, affection for the Supreme Lord is the most important. Only through associating with devotees of this quality can one hope to attain love for Krishna.

By way of contrast, someone who makes a show of love for Krishna while harboring desires for personal profit or fame, for liberation from material entanglement, or to some other end, is engaged in a deceitful bit of play-acting. Actions based on love for oneself or one's own senses cannot be honored by the name of love of God. Love means seeking the pleasure of another's senses, and only a devotee who has this mentality can be considered a great soul or mahat. Such a devotee is a part of the internal energy of the Lord and his mercy is effective in awakening love for Krishna in others.

DIFFERENT DEGREES *of* DEVOTEES

In the Chaitanya Charitamrita, Satyaraj Khan of Kulia village asked Mahaprabhu to explain the distinctions between the least advanced Vaishnavas, those who were more advanced, and those who were most advanced. This was the Lord's answer:

prabhu kahe vaiṣṇava-sevā nāma-saṅkīrtana
dui kara śīghra pābe śrī-kṛṣṇa-caraṇa

You should both serve the Vaishnavas and chant the Holy Name of Krishna. If you do these two things, you will quickly attain the shelter of Krishna's lotus feet. *CC 2.16.70*

prabhu kahe jāṅra mukhe śuni eka-bāra
kṛṣṇa-nāma sei pūjya śreṣṭha sabākāra

If I hear someone chant Krishna's Holy Name just once, I consider him to be worshipable and the best of all humans. *CC 2.15.106*

kṛṣṇa-nāma nirantara yāṅhāra vadane
sei vaiṣṇava-śreṣṭha bhaja tāṅhāra caraṇe

A person who is always chanting the Holy Name of the Lord is to be considered a first-class Vaishnava. Worship his lotus feet. *CC 2.16.72*

yāṅhāra darśane mukhe āise kṛṣṇa-nāma
tāṅhāre jāniha tumi vaiṣṇava-pradhāna

> One whose very sight brings the name of Krishna to your lips should be recognized as the best of all Vaishnavas.
> CC 2.16.74

These are the signs of the different degrees of Vaishnavas who cultivate the practice of chanting the Holy Name. Though all of them are holy, one should still discriminate for the purpose of choosing the ideal association for making spiritual advancement. One who knows fully the means and end of devotional service as described both in the teachings to Rupa and Sanatan, and in the conversations with Ramananda Raya, and who both practices and preaches them, is the true saint whose association is most desirable.

The ultimate example of devotional association was shown by Maharaj Parikshit. On learning that he would die in seven days, he undertook a fast in the company of Shukadeva, the best of the devotee Bhagavatas, and listened to him speak the book Bhagavatam with rapt attention until the fateful moment arrived.

The path followed by the great authorities, the Mahajanas, is the one that we should take. *Mahājano yena gataḥ sa panthā*. The Srimad Bhagavatam (6.3.20) says that there are twelve such great authorities: Brahma, Narada, Shiva, the four Kumaras, Kapila, Manu, Prahlada, Janaka, Bhishma, Bali, Shuka and Yamaraj. Each one of them, in his own way, demonstrated a particular way of achieving the perfection of devotion.

Without serving these twelve, or others like Markandeya, Ambarish, Vasu, Vyasa, Vibhishan, Pundarika, Vidura, Dhruva, Dalbhya, or Parashar, one is bound to commit great offenses. These supplementary names are found in the Padma Purana, which is quoted in *Laghu-bhāgavatamṛta* (2.2)—

mārkaṇḍeyo'mbarīṣaś ca
vasur vyāso vibhīṣaṇaḥ
puṇḍarīko baliḥ śambhuḥ
prahlādo viduro dhruvaḥ
dālbhyaḥ parāśaro bhīṣmo
nāradādyāś ca vaiṣṇavaiḥ
sevyā hariṁ niṣevyāmī no
ced āgaḥ paraṁ bhavet

The *Bṛhad-bhāgavatāmṛta* describes Prahlada as superior to Ambarish and other pure devotees (see SB 7.9.26), the Pandavas as superior to Prahlada (SB 7.10.50), the Yadavas as better than the Pandavas, and Uddhava as the best among the Yadavas (11.14.15). The Lord even says in the Bhagavatam (3.4.31) that Uddhava is in no way inferior to Him. Nevertheless, Uddhava himself admits that the gopis are superior to him—

āsām aho caraṇa-reṇu-juṣām ahaṁ syām
vṛndāvane kim api gulma-latauṣadhīnām
yā dustyajaṁ sva-janam ārya-pathaṁ ca hitvā
bhejur mukunda-padavīṁ śrutibhir vimṛgyām

> Ah, would that I could become one of Vrindavan's herbs and plants, all of which are regularly sprinkled with the dust of the gopis' feet! No one is superior to the gopis, who abandoned both their families and their religious principles, both of which are extremely difficult to give up, in order to worship Mukunda, the ultimate objective of all the Vedic literatures. SB 10.47.61

The Adi Purana states that the gopis are superior to the goddesses of fortune both in Vaikuntha and Dwaraka. And amongst the gopis, no one is superior to Radha. And just as Radha is most dear to the Lord, so is Her pond, Radha Kund.

yathā rādhā priyā viṣṇos
tasyāḥ kuṇḍaṁ priyaṁ tathā
sarva-gopīṣu sevaikā
viṣṇor atyanta-vallabhā

> Just as Radha is dear to Krishna, so too is Her pond, Radha Kund. Of all the gopis, She alone is supremely dear to Krishna.

Any devotee who is exclusively dedicated to Srimati Radharani, the daughter of King Vrishabhanu, without any ulterior motive, is the highest saint and his association is most desirable.

CHAPTER 10

Love *for* Krishna Comes *through* Rupanuga Vaishnavas

LOVE *for* CHANTING *the* HOLY NAME *is the* ROAD *to the* LORD'S INTIMATE PASTIMES

Srila Krishna Das Kaviraj wrote his account of Lord Chaitanya's ecstasies on the basis of eye witness descriptions given by Swarup Damodar Goswami and Raghunath Das Goswami. Though his Chaitanya Charitamrita gives only a tiny idea of the Lord's infinite and ineffable pastimes, it nevertheless allows us to get a picture of His last days in this world, when He was most deeply immersed in His mood of divine love in separation. The Lord, absorbed in Radharani's love for Krishna, spent the last twelve years of His manifest pastimes in the Gambhira, displaying the highest experience of love, known as *divyonmāda*. All this was not poetic imagining on the part of Krishna Das, but a faithful repetition of what he had heard directly from Swarup Damodar Goswami, who had seen it all with his own eyes.

Swarup Damodar was the Lord's inseparable companion during His last days. While the Lord was overwhelmed day and night by the madness of divine love, prattling seemingly senseless phrases, Swarup Damodar and Ramananda Raya alone were able to understand His inner mood, and they alone could help Him find peace of mind by singing songs or reciting poetry that matched this mood. These songs and poems came from five principal sources: those written by the Bengali poet Chandi Das, others written in Maithili by the poet Vidyapati, Jayadeva's Sanskrit songs and verses from the *Gīta-govinda*, Bilvamangala's *Kṛṣṇa-karṇāmṛta*, and Ramananda's own original compositions such as *Jagannātha-vallabha-nāṭaka*.

caṇḍī-dāsa vidyāpati
rāyera nāṭaka gīti
karṇāmṛta śrī-gīta-govinda
mahāprabhu rātri dine
svarūpa-rāmānandera sane
nāce gāya parama ānanda

> Mahaprabhu spent all His days and nights with Swarup Damodar and Ramananda Raya, dancing in ecstasy and singing the songs of Chandi Das and Vidyapati, Ramananda Raya's plays and songs, the *Kṛṣṇa-karṇāmṛta* and *Śrī Gīta-govinda*. CC 2.2.77

The Lord relished these poems in the company of His closest associates, but when ordinary people with a mundane mind-set try to imitate Him and enter into the mood of this transcendental literature, they nearly always end up with unintended consequences that are less than salutary. On the other hand, when one has attained a high level of spiritual realization, texts like these, which deal with the most elevated nectar of devotion, are the only ones that interest the practitioner. For this reason, one must try to develop the qualifications for such a culture through the practice of devotion in the association of advanced Vaishnavas. If one artificially attempts to do so while still in an immature stage of development, then his spiritual life will inevitably be compromised.

The proper procedure in the discipline of devotion is given by Bhaktivinode Thakur:

vidhi-mārga-rata jane svādhīnatā ratna dāne
rāga-mārge karān praveśa
rāga-vaśavartī haiyā pārakīya bhāvāśraye
labhe jīva kṛṣṇa-premāveśa

> To the practitioner of devotion who is fixed in the regulative principles, the Holy Name bestows the jewel of independence, placing him on the path of spontaneous devotion. Once overcome by spontaneous attachment to the Lord, the practitioner then takes shelter of the *parakīyā* mood and goes on to become absorbed in love for Krishna.
>
> *Kalyāna-Kalpa-Taru*

It is thus incumbent on the practitioner to chant the Holy Names with respect and affection on a daily basis until the Holy Name mercifully responds and blesses him with the ability to enter a realm that is inaccessible by any other means.

prati dina jadi ādara kariyā
se nāma kīrtana kari
sitopala jena nāśi roga-mūla
krame svādu haya hari

> If one affectionately and respectfully chants the Holy Name every single day, then it will destroy the roots of our material disease and gradually become relishable, just as sugar candy taken daily gradually becomes tasty to one afflicted with jaundice. *Śaraṇāgati*

īṣat vikaśi punaḥ dekhāya nija-rūpa-guṇa
citta hari laya kṛṣṇa pāśa
pūrṇa vikaśita hañā vraje more jāya lañā
dekhāya nija svarūpa vilāsa

> When the flower of the Holy Name has blossomed even slightly, it shows me its own spiritual form and characteristics. It steals my mind and takes me to Krishna's side. When the Name is in full bloom, it takes me directly to Vraja, where it shows me my personal role in the eternal pastimes.
>
> *Kṛṣṇa-nāma dhare kata bala? Śaraṇāgati*

Out of His unlimited love for His creatures, the Supreme Lord has appeared in this world in the form of His own Holy Name. By so doing, He has in effect made us all heirs to the kingdom of divine love and all the riches of spiritual perfection, but how can anyone expect to have the ability to understand or relish this great wealth without first having developed a taste for the chanting of the Holy Name?

Sri Chaitanya Mahaprabhu instructed His students in the chanting of the Holy Name, as told by Vrindavan Das Thakur in the Chaitanya Bhagavata:

> The Lord said: "Listen joyfully to the great mantra composed of Krishna's Names:

Hare Krishna Hare Krishna
Krishna Krishna Hare Hare
Hare Rama Hare Rama
Rama Rama Hare Hare.

prabhu kahe kahilām ei mahā-mantra
ihā giye japa sadā kariyā nirbandha
ihā haite sarva-siddhi haibe sabāra
sarva-kṣaṇa bala ithe vidhi nāhi āra

> I have spoken the Maha Mantra. Now go ahead and chant it (*japa*), being sure to take a vow to repeat it a fixed number of times every day. All perfections will come to you from chanting the Holy Name. Chant always; you need follow no other rule." *Cbh 2.23.75, 78*

In these two couplets spoken by the Lord, the first stresses the path of rules, the *vidhi-mārga*, while the second indicates the path of spontaneous attachment, or the *rāga-mārga*.

The word *japa* in the first verse is defined as *hṛdy uccāre*, or repeating the sacred syllables with heart or emotion. Japa can be of three kinds: *vācika*, meaning loud enough that anyone can hear; *mānasika*, or chanting mentally; and *upāṁśu*, which means whispered in a way that only the chanter himself can hear.

The word *nirbandha* found in the first couplet also has a number of meanings. It refers to fixed concentration, unity of thought and action, enthusiasm, determination to achieve the desired goal, and affectionate respect for the practice, in this case the chanting of the Holy Name. Moreover, it refers to the commitment to chant a fixed number of Holy Names every day.

Sri Chaitanya Mahaprabhu used to say that He would only accept invitations to eat in the homes of the rich. When his poorer disciples expressed dismay that they would thus be forever deprived of having Him in their homes, He would laugh and say that He meant rich in the Holy Names through repeating them a hundred thousand times each day. In this way He indicated that a hundred thousand repetitions of the Holy Name each day is the threshold that all of His followers should try to achieve.

However, this does not mean that one should simply chant in an attempt to fulfill one's vow of chanting a certain number of Names. If one does so, then *ādara*, the principle of affectionate respect for the Holy Name, will be adversely affected. One must pronounce the Holy Name clearly and with feeling. This will result in quickly experiencing positive results from chanting.

VAISHNAVA ASSOCIATION WILL HELP OVERCOME OFFENSES

There once was a Vaishnava king in Vishnupur named Gopal Singh. This Gopal Singh ordered all his subjects to chant a lakh every single day. Naturally, most people were not altogether enthusiastic about chanting after a long and hard day's work. Thus the Bengali expression was born "Gopal Singh's *begāra*," which is applied to any religious activity done under duress. If one chants the Holy Name in this way, it is certain that nothing much will ever come of it.

bahu janma kare jadi śravaṇa kīrtana
tabu to nā pāya kṛṣṇa-pade prema-dhana

> One may engage in the devotional service of chanting and hearing for many lifetimes and still not attain love for Krishna. *CC 1.8.16*

Srila Bhaktivinode Thakur comments in the *Amṛta-pravāha-bhāṣya*: "A person who commits the ten types of offenses to the Holy Name may hear and chant for many lifetimes without finding love for Krishna."

The ten offenses to the Holy Name are our principal misfortune, which we can escape with the assistance of pure Vaishnavas. Bhaktivinode Thakur sets the example of how to call out with emotion for the bountiful association of Vaishnavas attached to Krishna's Holy Name in his classic song, *Ohe Vaiṣṇava Ṭhākura !*

ekākī āmāya nāhi pāya bala,
hari-nāma-saṅkīrtane
tumi kṛpā kori' śraddhā-bindu diyā
deho kṛṣṇa-nāma-dhane

> Alone, I do not have the strength to perform Harinam sankirtan. Please be kind and give me a single drop of faith. Please bestow upon me the priceless treasure of Krishna's Name!

kṛṣṇa se tomāra kṛṣṇa dite pāro,
tomāra śakati āche
āmi to kāṅgāla kṛṣṇa kṛṣṇa boli',
dhāi tava pāche pāche

> Krishna belongs to you. You thus have the power to give me Krishna! I am nothing more than a beggar running behind you, calling out His Names, 'Krishna! Krishna!' *Śaraṇāgati*

Krishna mercifully appears in this material world in the form of the spiritual master simply to rain down blessings on poor unfortunate souls like us. How can we ever get His mercy without first receiving the blessings of the spiritual master and the other Vaishnavas, who are oceans of mercy and filled with compassion for the suffering souls of this world?

Narottam Das Thakur has also sung the praises of Vaishnava association:

ki rūpe pāiba sevā mui durācāra
śrī-guru-vaiṣṇave rati nā haila āmāra

> How can a wicked soul like myself attain service to the Lord? I have no affection for the service of the spiritual master and the Vaishnavas.

aśeṣa māyāte mon magana hoilo
vaiṣṇavete leśa-mātra rati nā janmilo

> My mind has remained merged in the unlimited world of illusion and has not developed even a drop of attachment for the company of the Vaishnavas.

viṣaye bhuliyā andha hainu divā-niśi
gale phāṅsa dite phire māyā se piśācī

> I have totally forgotten myself in sense gratification and have become blind, both day and night. In the meantime, that witch Maya follows me around, looking for a chance to place a noose around my neck.

māyāre kariyā joy chāṛāno nā jāy
sādhu kṛpā vinā āra nāhiko upāy

There seems to be no way that I can get free of her. Other than the mercy of the saintly, there is nothing that can help me to conquer over Maya.

adoṣa-daraśi prabhu patita uddhār
ei bāra narottame karaha nistār

O Master, you see no fault in anyone, you deliver even the most fallen. The time has now come to save Narottam Das.

Krishna Das Kaviraj further describes the means of showing submission to the Vaishnavas and getting their blessings—

bhakta-pada-dhūli āra bhakta-pada-jala
bhakta-bhukta-avaśeṣa tina mahā-bala
ei tina-sevā haite kṛṣṇa-premā haya
punaḥ punaḥ sarva-śāstre phukāriyā kaya
tāte bāra bāra kahi śuna bhakta-gaṇa
viśvāsa kariyā kara e-tina sevana
tina haite kṛṣṇa-nāma-premera ullāsa
kṛṣṇera prasāda tāte sākṣī kālidāsa

Three things give strength to one's spiritual practices: the dust of the devotees' lotus feet, the water that has washed their feet and the remnants of their food. All the revealed scriptures loudly proclaim over and over again that one can attain the supreme goal of ecstatic love for Krishna through the use of these three substances. So, my dear devotees, please listen to me, for I insist on this point: keep faith in these three things and render service to them with complete faith. Through these three substances you will taste the joy of sacred love that is found in the Holy Name of Krishna and you will win Krishna's pleasure. This has been proved by the experience of Kali Das. *CC 3.16.58-63*

Krishna Das wrote these verses as the conclusion to his narrative of Kali Das, an uncle of Raghunath Das Goswami who received Sri Chaitanya Mahaprabhu's extraordinary blessings. Kali Das was extremely devoted to the chanting of the Holy Name, but over and beyond this, he sought out the remnants of Vaishnavas' meals and took the dust of their feet or the water that had washed their feet wherever he could, even from devotees who were of low social standing or caste. Mahaprabhu later allowed Kali Das to drink the water that had washed His own feet, something He rarely allowed anyone else to do. Thus Krishna Das glorified these three things as the means of getting Krishna's mercy and the joy of ecstatic love for Krishna.

Sri Chaitanya Mahaprabhu came to give Krishna prema, the highest and unequalled goal of human life. He revealed the glories of Krishna's pastimes in Vrindavan and Radharani's love for the Lord. Prabodhananda Saraswati glorifies Him with the following words:

premā nāmādbhutārthaḥ
śravaṇa-patha-gataḥ
kasya nāmnāṁ mahimnaḥ
ko vettā kasya vṛndāvana-vipina-mahā-
mādhurīṣu praveśaḥ
ko vā jānāti rādhāṁ parama-rasa-camat-
kāra-mādhurya-sīmām
ekaś caitanya-candraḥ parama-karuṇayā
sarvam āviścakāra

Before the rising of the Chaitanya moon, who had ever heard that prema was the fifth and highest goal of human life? And who knew fully the glories of the Holy Name? And who knew how to enter into the sweet pastimes of the Lord in the forest bowers of Vrindavan? And who knew the extent of Radharani's sweet and glorious mood of divine love in the conjugal mood? Indeed, until the generous Lord appeared as Chaitanya Mahaprabhu to display His unequalled mercy and reveal these secrets, no one.

Caitanya-candrāmṛta 112

At the end of the fifth chapter of his book, *Śrīman Mahāprabhura Śikṣā,* Srila Bhaktivinode Thakur quotes this verse and comments: "Prior to the coming of Sri Chaitanya, no one had ever had an inkling of the divine experiences that He would reveal."

RUPA GOSWAMI: *The* INCARNATION *of* MAHAPRABHU'S MERCY

Srila Rupa Goswami was the incarnation of Mahaprabhu's love and mercy. The Lord invested him with spiritual power and the ability to understand His teachings about Krishna, devotion, and the experience of the Lord's transcendental personality in love. Rupa thus became the greatest expert on these most confidential aspects of spiritual life and doctrine. Of course, he was Mahaprabhu's eternal companion and not an ordinary conditioned soul. His inner identity is that of Rupa Manjari, Srimati Radharani's beloved maidservant. Thus, who but he could know in intimate detail the desires of the Lord and the profound purpose of His incarnation? Narottam Das Thakur in his *Prārthanā* prayers first utters a heartfelt appeal to Rupa and Raghunath Das Goswami for the ability to understand and enter into the conjugal pastimes of the Divine Couple. He prays:

śrī rūpa mañjarī pada sei mora sampada
sei mora bhajana-pūjana
sei mora prāṇa-dhana sei more ābharaṇa
sei mora jīvanera jīvana

Sri Rupa Manjari's feet are my only possession. They are my religious practice, my worship. They are my wealth; they are my ornament, the life of my life.

With verses like these, Narottam Das established clearly that Rupa Goswami above all others revealed the inner purpose of Lord Chaitanya's incarnation. He therefore feelingly prayed to Rupa Goswami to be allowed to enter into the Lord's pastimes. Similarly, Krishna Das Kaviraj ends every single chapter of the Chaitanya Charitamrita with a prayer to Rupa and Raghunath—

śrī-rūpa-raghunātha-pade jāra āśa
caitanya-caritāmṛta kahe kṛṣṇa-dāsa

Krishna Das, whose one hope is to attain the lotus feet of Sri Rupa and Raghunath, recounts the nectarean biography of Chaitanya Mahaprabhu.

Bhaktivinode Thakur, the greatest follower of Rupa and Raghunath in the 19th century, echoed this prayer in his songs—

hā rūpa gosāñi dayā kari kobe
dibe dīne vraja vāsā
rāgātmika tumi tava padānuga
haite dāsera āśā

O Rupa Goswami! When will you be merciful and give me residence in the land of Vraja ? You possess spontaneous love for the Divine Couple. This servant of yours wishes only to follow in your footsteps. *Śaraṇāgati, Bhajana-lālasā 9*

śrī-rūpa-mañjarī saṅge jābo kabe
rasa sevā śikṣā tare
tad-anugā haye rādhā-kuṇḍa taṭe
rahibo harṣitāntare

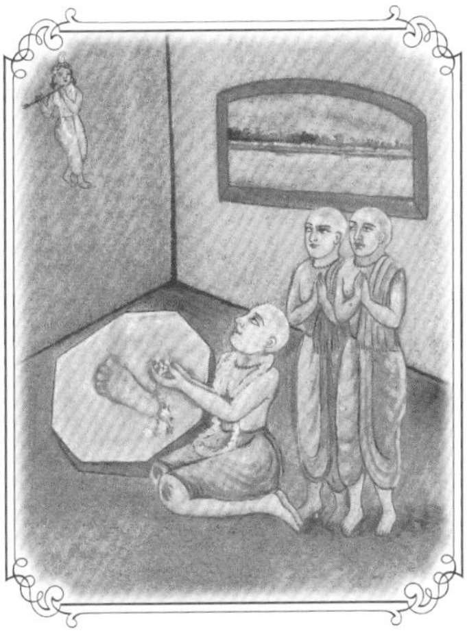

When will I go take the association of Rupa Manjari to learn about how to serve the Divine Couple intimately? Becoming her follower, I will live forever on the banks of Radha Kund, my heart overflowing with joy.

Gīta-mālā, Siddha-lālasā 4

Our spiritual master, Srila Bhaktisiddhanta Saraswati Thakur, follows in the current of devotion in the mood of Rupa Goswami that was thus released by Bhaktivinode Thakur. His entire earthly pastime was living proof of this. His final teachings show his dedication to Sri Sri Rupa and Raghunath:

"All of you please preach the message of Rupa and Raghunath with great enthusiasm. The ultimate object of our desires is to become specks of dust at the lotus feet of those who follow Sri Rupa Goswami....

"We do not seek to become heroes performing great works or religious deeds; our true being and identity is to be a speck of dust at the lotus feet of Sri Rupa Prabhu, lifetime after lifetime. The stream that flows from Srila Bhaktivinode Thakur will never be dammed up. Remember this and vow to double your efforts to fulfill Srila Bhaktivinode Thakur's desires....

"We seek nothing for ourselves; our only motto is:

ādadānas tṛṇaṁ dantair
idaṁ yāce punaḥ punaḥ
śrīmad-rūpa-padāmbhoja-
dhūliḥ syāṁ janma-janmani

Taking grass between my teeth, I pray repeatedly that I may become a speck of dust at Sri Rupa Goswami's lotus feet, birth after birth."

Raghunatha Das Goswami, Muktā-carita

The Supreme Lord appeared in His form as Lord Chaitanya Mahaprabhu in this age of quarrel and hypocrisy to give something that He had never given in any previous epoch—the most effulgent and sweetly intimate love for Himself. His dearmost servant Srila Rupa Goswami was heir to this divine power and teaching, and no part of the Lord's purpose or pastimes remained hidden from him. Without the mercy of Rupa Goswami, therefore, no one will attain the qualifications needed to enter into this confidential realm. Our spiritual masters similarly participate in these munificent pastimes of the Lord, following in the footsteps of Srila Rupa Goswami. Our hearts are as dry as the desert, but they will flood them with the nectar of devotion if we sincerely adhere to their lotus feet.

Srila Prabhupada called the *Śikṣāṣṭakam,* the only text composed by Sri Chaitanya Mahaprabhu, and Rupa Goswami's *Upadeśāmṛtam*, the best guides to the path of devotional spirituality. By publishing commentaries on both these works,[7] Srila Prabhupada further elucidated the path to spiritual perfection. Anyone who follows their guidance will attain the supreme goal of ecstatic love for Krishna, and by so doing achieve the highest levels of holiness.

[1] See the commentary to Srimad Bhagavatam 5.19.26.

[2] *mahat-sevayā yādṛcchika-mahat-kṛpā-janitayā mahatāṁ sevayā śraddadhānasya jāta-śraddhayā puṁsaḥ puṇya-tīrthaṁ sad-gurus tasya niṣevaṇaṁ caraṇāśrayaṇaṁ syāt nidānāgamayos tīrtham ṛṣi-juṣṭa-jale gurāv ity amaraḥ tasmāc ca śuśrūṣos tasya vāsudeva-kathāsu ruciḥ syāt.*

[3] *mad-anugraha eva kadā syāt ? tatrāha he abja-nābha ! sad-upāsanayā hetunā yarhi tvayi matiḥ syāt sad-upāsanaiva kadā syāt ? tatrāha puṁso yarhi saṁsaraṇasya saṁsārasya apavargaḥ anta-kālaḥ syāt saṁsārānta-kāla eva kadā syāt ? iti cet, yadā yādṛcchikī sat-kṛpā syād iti jñeyam tenādau yādṛcchikī sat-kṛpā tataḥ saṁsāra-nāśārambhas, tataḥ sad-upāsanā, tataḥ kṛṣṇe matir iti kramaḥ.*

[4] *nanu mat-kṛpāṁ vinā sat-saṅgamo'pi na syāt ity ato mat-kṛpaivādi-kāraṇam astu ? tatrāha – santa eva gatir āśrayo yasya tasmin svecchāmayasya* [BhP 10.14.2] *iti, ahaṁ bhakta-parādhīnaḥ* [BhP 9.4.63] *ity ādeḥ sad-icchayaiva tava sarvaṁ pravartate na svata iti budhyate atas tvat-kṛpāpi sad-anugataiveti bhāvaḥ satāṁ gatāv ity asminn arthe' py asatāṁ gatir na bhavasīti pūrva-pūrveṇa satāṁ parasparasya sattve niṣpādita eva tvat-kṛpā pravartate, na tu pūrvaṁ svayaṁ samuttīrya* [BhP 10.2.31] *ity āder ity eṣā.*

[5] This same verse appears with slightly different wording in the last line in both the *Muṇḍaka Upaniṣad* (2.2.9) and Eleventh Canto (11.20.30). Of the three versions, this one is the most directly theistic in its language.

[6] The Chaitanya Charitamrita changes the order of these items somewhat. In the original *Bhakti-rasāmṛta-sindhu*, the five activities are given in the following order: serving the Deity, hearing the Bhagavatam, associating with devotees, chanting the Holy Names and living in Mathura. This reading is confirmed from other editions of Chaitanya Charitamrita, though some editions follow the *Bhakti-rasāmṛta-sindhu* version.

[7] B. P. Puri Maharaj writes: "We had the good fortune to see the first edition of this book, which was printed in 1928 from the Gaudiya Printing Works on Upper Circular Road in Calcutta."

About the Author

Vaishnava Sarvabhauma Sri Srila Bhakti Promode Puri Goswami Maharaj

In the early years of this century, Srila Prabhupada Bhaktisiddhanta Saraswati Goswami Thakur set into motion a devotional revival that rapidly spread through Bengal, India, and eventually the world. He put into question the very foundations of present-day theistic thought in a way that has little comparison anywhere in the spiritual record, East or West. Through him, the world was awakened to the teachings of Sri Chaitanya Mahaprabhu and the movement of pure devotion, *śuddhā bhakti*.

In orchestrating this modern bhakti revolution, Srila Prabhupada gathered some of the greatest spiritual luminaries in contemporary history into his circle. Such a convergence of exalted spiritual personalities can only be compared to the coming together of Sri Chaitanya's direct followers in the sixteenth century. One of the devotional giants who entered Srila Prabhupada's orbit was the author of this book, His Divine Grace Srila Bhakti Promode Puri Goswami Maharaj.

We cannot describe the life of Srila Puri Goswami Maharaj without emphasizing his contribution to the spiritual movement in which he was so integrally involved. The depth of his accomplishments cannot be fathomed outside the context of Sri Gaudiya Math. With his fellow godbrothers, he shared an indomitable faith in the service of his Guru and the message of Sri Chaitanya Mahaprabhu. This service was the sole purpose and highest aspiration of his being. This conviction led him to spend his entire life in the pursuit of Srila Prabhupada and Mahaprabhu's pleasure and the fulfillment of their desires. If we examine his life in this setting, we will see more than just numbers, dates, places and names. We will see how he embodied the very life current that his spiritual preceptors came to give the world.

Srila Puri Goswami Maharaj took birth in the village of Ganganandapur in Jessore district (in present-day Bangladesh), on October 8, 1898. His parents, Tarini Charan Chakravarti and Srimati Ram Rangini Devi, named him Sri Promode Bhushan Chakravarti. During his childhood, he met his *vartma-pradarśaka* guru ("one who opens the door to the path of devotion"), Srila Bhakti Ratna Thakur, a godbrother and siksha disciple of Thakur Bhaktivinoda, the legendary architect of the present Gaudiya Vaishnava movement. Through Bhakti Ratna Thakur he was introduced to *Sajjana-toṣaṇī*, Bhaktivinoda Thakur's own Vaishnava periodical, which was filled with Bhaktivinoda's commentaries and holy teachings. In this way Srila Puri Maharaj became familiar with the seminal works of the śuddhā bhakti tradition, such as Chaitanya Charitamrita, Chaitanya Bhagavata and the Srimad Bhagavatam. It was also through Bhakti Ratna Thakur that he first learned of his future guru, Srila Bhaktisiddhanta Saraswati Goswami Prabhupada.

Srila Puri Maharaj was still a young university student when he first came before Srila

Prabhupada at the Yoga Pith in Sri Mayapur in 1915. It was a significant occasion, for Srila Prabhupada's diksha guru, Paramahamsa Thakur Srimad Gaura Kishor Das Babaji, had entered his eternal abode only the day before. Srila Puri Maharaj often recounted that as soon as he saw Srila Prabhupada and paid his obeisances to him for the first time, he knew in his heart that this was his spiritual master. Some years later, on the auspicious day of Sri Krishna Janmastami in 1923, he accepted both Harinam and mantra diksha from Srila Prabhupada and was given the name Pranavananda Brahmachari.

At the time, Sri Gaudiya Math was rapidly establishing itself as a bona fide manifestation of Indian religious culture and transforming the caste-conscious socio-religious world of Hinduism. Srila Prabhupada Saraswati Thakur was bringing together his intimate associates to share the wealth of Sri Krishna sankirtan. He had accepted tridandi sannyasa in 1918 and by the early 1920's had already assumed a formidable position in the Bengali spiritual firmament. He was fearless when it came to upholding true religious principles. The students and practitioners of the Gaudiya Math aligned themselves with this attitude and led most exemplary lives of devotion, imbued with austerity, discipline and in-depth scriptural learning. This high standard of religious life was the hallmark of Sri Gaudiya Math and would be the thread that guided all of Srila Prabhupada's disciples, including Srimad Puri Goswami Maharaj.

The keystone of success in devotion is to perfectly hear the holy words spoken by one's spiritual preceptor. Srila Prabhupada would often say, "All that is required of you is that you lend me your ears." Srila Puri Maharaj was fully committed to this maxim. He had the great good fortune to associate closely with Srila Prabhupada for thirteen years and during that time he served him personally by recording his lectures and conversations, which were later published. The greater part of Srila Prabhupada's spoken words we are left with today come from the transcriptions of these notes. At the same time, Srila Puri Maharaj cultivated a deep knowledge of the Vaishnava scriptures, with the result that he became a veritable storehouse of the wealth of the preceptorial line coming from Sri Chaitanya and his followers. This led him to become one of the most prolific writers and influential teachers in all of Gaudiya Vaishnava history. His writings reflect the disciplined eye of a scholar who expresses with grace and directness the purest scriptural conclusions supported by his own uncommonly profound realization.

Following Srila Prabhupada's directives, our Gurudeva edited, wrote for, published and helped distribute countless spiritual publications. He was initially inspired and directed by Srila Prabhupada to start writing and contributing articles to the *Gauḍīya* magazine, the backbone of the Gaudiya Math's missionary work. For seven years he served as a proofreader and as one of its primary editors. In 1926, he was charged with running the world's only daily Vaishnava newspaper, *Dainika Nadiyā Prakāśa.* He held this service for two years, publishing all of his preceptor's daily discourses along with articles by fellow students and other contemporaries. His service and learning did not pass unnoticed by Srila Prabhupada who awarded him the titles of *mahā-mahopadeśaka* ("great instructor") and *pratna-vidyālaṅkāra* ("keeper of the wisdom of the ancient scriptural lore").

After the disappearance of his Gurudeva in 1937, Srila Puri Maharaj continued his vocation of spreading the teachings of Sri Chaitanya through the Gauḍīya magazine, first out of the Bagh Bazaar Gaudiya Math and then later the Sri Chaitanya Math in Mayapur. After he founded the Sri Chaitanya Gaudiya Math, Srila Puri Goswami Maharaj's godbrother, Srimad Bhakti Dayita Madhava Maharaj, invited him to head the editorial board of *Chaitanya Vāṇī* magazine in 1964. Puri Maharaj served in this capacity for thirty-three years, furthering his life's work of preserving the teachings of his spiritual lineage. Through *Chaitanya Vāṇī*, he continued to make a deep impact on the devotional world.

In all, our venerable teacher's wisdom is embodied in over sixty years of writings on Vaishnava philosophy and theology. He penned a rich variety of texts, bringing the Bhagavata dharma to life through hundreds of poems, essays, narratives, diaries, editorials and personal letters, thus creating a storehouse of the wealth of pure devotion for his disciples and the world at large.

In 1942, Srila Prabhupada appeared to Srila Puri Maharaj in a dream vision and imparted to him the sannyas mantra, ordering him to accept the renounced order. After accepting tridaṇḍī-sannyāsa from his godbrother Bhakti Gaurava Vaikhanasa Maharaj in Champahati in August of 1946, he toured parts of India with other godbrothers such as Bhakti Hridoy Bon Maharaj and Bhakti Dayita Madhava Maharaj. In the meantime, he continued to write and lecture with dedication. At the behest of his godbrother Tridandi Swami Bhakti Vilasa Tirtha Maharaj, he also served for seven years as chief pujari for the Yoga Pith temple, the birthsite of Sri Chaitanya Mahaprabhu.

Srila Puri Maharaj took up a more solitary life of worship in the 1950's. He moved to a humble cottage on the banks of the Ganges in Ambika Kalna. The king of Burdwan was extremely impressed by his saintly ascetic character and, on the appearance day of Srimati Radharani in 1958, presented him with the ancient Ananta Vasudeva temple in Kalna.

In 1989, at the age of 91, Srila Puri Goswami Maharaj established the Sri Gopinath Gaudiya Math in Ishodyan, Sri Mayapur, for the service of their divine lordships, Sri Sri Gaura-Gadadhar, Jagannath Deva, Radha-Gopinath and Lakshmi-Narasingha Deva. In the following years, he established other temples in Jagannath Puri, Vrindavan, Calcutta and Midnapore.

Srila Puri Maharaj taught through his every action. He excelled in all aspects of devotional practice and there was perhaps no area in which he did not exhibit utmost expertise, diligence and foresight. This ranged from his encyclopedic knowledge of scripture, to maintaining the printing press, to his beautiful singing of kirtan. He was especially recognized for his sensitivity and attention to detail in the performance of deity worship and devotional rites and was thus widely called upon to be the head priest in most of the Gaudiya Math's deity installations and ceremonial functions. He was rarely known to rest; his service was an uninterrupted flow. Even in his later years, he would remain awake, writing and chanting through the night while all his youthful disciples were still asleep. When his personal servants came in the morning, they would inevitably find him awake and chanting the Holy Name, arisen before everyone else in the ashram.

Srila Bhakti Promode Puri Maharaj had outstanding love for his godbrothers and was inspired in his glorification of others. He found richness in everyone he met. He had the quality of making one feel so much wanted and their life so much valued. At the same time, he paid the least attention to himself. He was an emblem of humility and simplicity, and his generosity of spirit and kindness touched the hearts of the whole Vaishnava community. Among his lifetime, intimate companions were Srila Bhakti Rakshak Sridhar Deva Goswami Maharaj, Srila Bhakti Prajnan Keshava Maharaj, and Srila Akinchan Krishna Das Babaji Maharaj. Toward the end of his sojourn in this world, he was honored by the Gaudiya Vaishnava community for his learning, long life of service and devotion and made president of the World Vaishnava Association in 1995.

"He has love for his Guru; and let it be known that his life is one with his words." This tribute, coming from Srila Prabhupada himself, is the most revealing statement about Srila Puri Goswami Maharaj's personality and qualities. He gave credit for all of his accomplishments to the mercy of his Gurudeva alone. Through the blessings of Srila Bhaktisiddhanta Saraswati Goswami Thakur, Srila Bhakti Promode Puri Maharaj attracted the hearts of so many to the Bhagavata religion. People from so many different backgrounds and countries found in him a true spiritual guide and shelter. He upheld the principles of pure Vaishnavism and delineated the path of sharanagati. He so embodied pure devotion and service to his spiritual master that one of his disciples once remarked that he was able to "silently lay down Srila Prabhupada's entire siddhanta."

We are greatly indebted to His Divine Grace for his gift–a lifetime of pure devotion, spanning over a century, which we can aspire for, learn from, and discuss about for our own spiritual nourishment. Srila Puri Maharaj departed this world for the eternal abode in the predawn hours of Narayan Chaturdasi, October 21, 1999, one day before the Rasa Purnima. His divine body was transported from Jagannath Puri to the Gopinath Gaudiya Math in Ishodyan and there placed in his eternal samadhi shrine. Prior to his departure from this world, Srila Puri Goswami Maharaj appointed his intimate disciple, Sripada Bhakti Bibudha Bodhayan Maharaj as his successor and President-acharya of Sri Gopinath Gaudiya Math.

In years to come, as more of his words and vision are translated, the world outside of Bengal and India will come to know the spirit of the true Vaishnava religion that he tirelessly shared. May the gentle rain of nectar of his perfect teachings continue to bring auspiciousness into this world.

PRESENTING *the* TEACHINGS *of* SWAMI B. P. PURI

PURI DARSHANS SERIES

This series of six informal *darshans*, or talks, was shared with students from around the world at the annual Rathayatra festival. The centenarian master of the tradition teaches the importance of closely following the path of *bhakti* in order to develop a proper conception and realization of the eternal world. VHS $19.95, DVD $21.95. Also available in PAL format.

Item AV3531 (VH or DV)

PART 1
Sambandha, Abhideya, Prayojana (A)

Item AV3532 (VH or DV)

PART 2
Sambandha, Abhideya, Prayojana (B)

Item AV3533 (VH or DV)

PART 3
First Deserve, Then Desire

Item AV3534 (VH or DV)

PART 4
Jagannath's All-seeing Eyes

Item AV3535 (VH or DV)

PART 5
Pitfalls on the Path of Devotion

Item AV3536 (VH or DV)

PART 6
Developing the Eye of Love

THE ART OF SADHANA VIDEO SERIES
VOLUMES 1 & 2

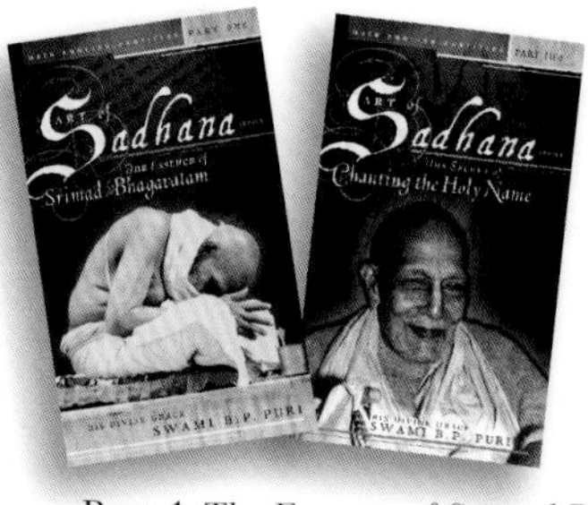

Original video recordings of Puri Maharaj in Vrindavan, India. The importance of the supreme Vedic literature, Srimad Bhagavatam, and the teachings of Saraswati Thakur are addressed in these captivating darshans.

Part 1: The Essence of Srimad Bhagavatam
68 min., Eng. subt., VHS $19.95, DVD $21.95

Part 2: The Secret of Chanting the Holy Name
62 min., Eng. subt., VHS $19.95, DVD $21.95

SAMADHI
SWAMI B.P. PURI

This official publication commemorates the completion of Swami B.P. Puri's samadhi mandir in Mayapur. Inside, an excerpt from Bodhayan Maharaj's forthcoming biography of his gurudev details his auspicious advent and boyhood pastimes. Further, articles by Bhaktivinode Thakur, Bhaktisiddhanta Saraswati Thakur and Puri Maharaj himself examine the true meaning of samadhi.

$24.95, cloth,
130pp, 7.25 x 9.75"

OF LOVE & SEPARATION

Meditations on My Divine Master

Includes a collection of personal reflections and remembrances that allow the reader to glimpse the divinity His Holiness experienced through real and untiring devotion to his guru.

Item 1413: $24.95
cloth, 160 pp, 8 x 10.5"

THE HEART OF KRISHNA

Revised Edition

The Heart of Krishna examines the pitfalls along the spiritual path, with a special emphasis on avoiding *vaishnava aparadha*, or offending devotees, especially pure devotees.

Item 1426: $14.95
paper, 1-886069-47-6,
80 color plates, 108 pp
7.5 x 10.25"

SRI VYASA PUJA

Bhagavata Dharma: 101 Years of Devotion

Sri Vyasa Puja contains many heartfelt offerings and devotional essays by disciples and well-wishers.

Item 1407: $12.95 cloth
Item 1407sb: $7.95 paper
72pp, color photographs,
10 x 11"

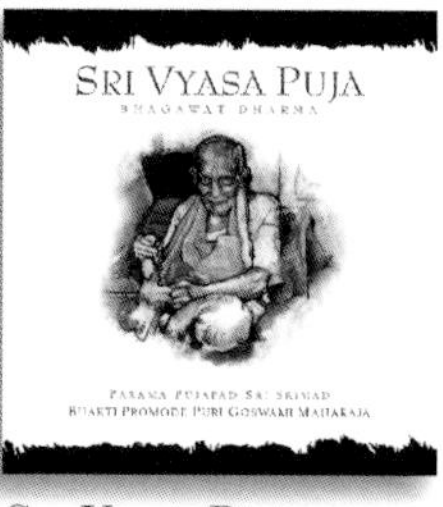

SRI VYASA PUJA

100 Years of Devotion

Celebrating the centennial appearance day of Swami B.P. Puri, *Sri Vyasa Puja* contains many heartfelt offerings and devotional essays by his students and well-wishers. Contains an autobiography written in his 100th year, as well as a potent article on the inner meaning of Rathayatra and the Holy Name.

Item 1420s; $ 9.95 paper,
72 pp, color photographs,
10 x 15"

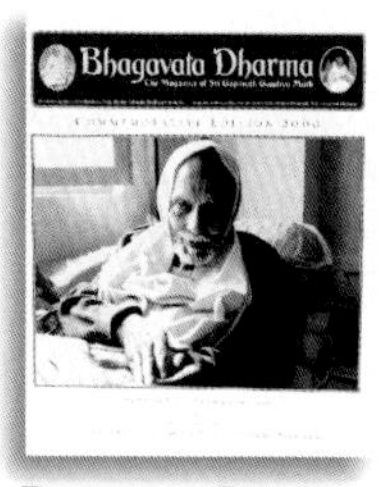

BHAGAVATA DHARMA

Commemorative Edition 2000

Offerings to His Divine Grace Srila Bhakti Promode Puri Goswami Maharaj

The 102nd Vyasa Puja and first Disappearance title, is filled with beautiful offerings of devotion unto Srila Bhakti Promode Puri Goswami Maharaj.

Item 1412: $12.95 paper,
128 pp, color photographs,
9 x 11"

THE ART OF SADHANA

A Guide to Daily Devotio

Art of Sadhana speaks about th importance of the inner mood of the servitor while engaging in religious practices. Includes essays on the worship of Sri Guru, regulative devotional practice, spontaneous loving devotion, and the proper chant of mantras and benefits derivec from them.

Item 1206: $19.95 cloth,
1-886069-02-6
Item 1206sb: $15.95 paper,
1-886069-03-4
257 pp, 9 x 10"